RED STAR OVER POLAND

RED STAR OVER POLAND

A Report From Behind The Iron Curtain

By

Edward S. Kerstein

With an Introduction by

SZYMON ST. DEPTULA
Dept. of Polish and Russian
University of Wisconsin

C. C. NELSON PUBLISHING COMPANY
Appleton, Wisconsin
1947

Jacket and Sketches by Reginald Hardie
Printed in U. S. A.

TO

MY BROTHER

ALOIS A. KERSTEIN,

TWICE WOUNDED IN THE ITALIAN CAMPAIGN OF WORLD
WAR II, FIGHTING WITH THE 91ST INFANTRY DIVISION
FOR THE LIBERATION OF NATIONS FROM TOTALITARIANISM
—BE IT BROWN OR RED.

In his message to Poland, broadcast on May 3, 1941, former British Prime Minister Winston Churchill said:

"Every day Hitler's firing parties are busy in a dozen lands. Monday he shoots Dutchmen; Tuesday, Norwegians; Wednesday, French and Belgians stand against the wall; Thursday, it is the Czechs who must suffer, and now there are the Serbs and the Greeks to fill his repulsive bill of execution. But always, all of the days, there are the Poles."

* * *

Expressing concern over millions of persons who had disappeared in the new Poland, Winston Churchill in a speech before the House of Commons on August 16, 1945, said:

"Guarded accounts of what has happened, and what is happening, have filtered through, but it is not impossible that tragedy on a prodigious scale is imposing itself behind the iron curtain which at present divides Europe in twain."

PREFACE

At dawn on September 1, 1939, German land, sea and air forces attacked Poland without any declaration of war, crossing the frontier at 14 points from East Prussia, West Prussia, Silesia, Moravia and Slovakia. Dive bombers poured destruction on all Polish airfields and 61 towns within the first few hours.

On September 5, 1939, American Ambassador Anthony J. Drexel Biddle, Jr., quit Warsaw as German bombs were falling on the Polish capital. A few weeks later he left the country. With his departure America lost direct diplomatic communication with Poland, which was not resumed until almost six years later. On July 31, 1945, another American ambassador, Arthur Bliss Lane, arrived in Warsaw, bringing an end to one of the most troublesome diplomatic problems growing out of the war.

For more than five years during the war the Polish government-in-exile in London had functioned as the true representative of Poland, and was recognized as such by most nations of the world, including Russia (from 1941 to 1943 when she broke off relations with the London government over the Katyn massacre of 10,000 Polish officers taken prisoner by the Soviets in the first month of the war when Russia invaded Poland from the East while Hitler was attacking the Poles in the North, West and South.) The London government did not return to Poland, however, at the close of the war. Instead, the Russian-sponsored Polish Committee for National Liberation proclaimed itself as the new Polish provisional government and was given recognition first by Russia and subsequently by the United States and Great Britain as a result of the Yalta Conference.

American and British recognition of the provisional government has become one of the most controversial postwar subjects. Opponents of the Polish government-in-exile in London contended that that government favored only the large landowners and did not represent the common folk of Poland, while opponents of the provisional government contended that that government was communistic, was subservient to Moscow and represented only a minority group.

On September 19, 1945, the new Polish provisional government granted clearance to *The Milwaukee Journal* for immediate entry of its representative in Poland. I was called in from the "police beat" and assigned for the trip because of my knowledge of Polish. I left for Poland the following day.

Speaking Polish fluently, I walked and lived with many of the average citizens of Poland and thus obtained first-hand information from them. I did not depend solely on the reports and statements of Polish government officials, but went deep into the Polish hinterland to get the story I tell.

Edward S. Kerstein

CONTENTS

INTRODUCTION

A REPORT FROM THE LAND OF CHAOS

Sometimes the thought is almost frightening when one considers the quality and the source of so many of our foreign journalists abroad, to be sure, but very frequently these career correspondents are wholly innocent of any knowledge of the language and the social, economic, political, and historical background of the land into which they are dispatched as observers, interpreters, and commentators. Obviously a man cannot be expected to know Italian thoroughly one year and cover that country for a season when next year he may be sent by his paper or syndicate to cover Japan or Argentina, equally unprepared linguistically and historically to do a first-rate job. We think it ridiculous when a foreigner comes to this country, makes a rapid transcontinental trip, and knowing relatively little English, yet returns home and "writes" us up. We would think that a thorough knowledge of the language and of the historical, political, economic, and social background of the country we are asked to pontificate about would constitute the very minimum required of any reporter whose accounts of day-by-day events and trends in the country that is his beat are to furnish us with the reliable information we have the right to expect from our responsible newspapers and syndicates.

Yet such is not too often the case with our own press representatives abroad. We assign a man like Larry Allen, a good man no doubt in Anglo-Saxon domain, but hardly a proper man to send out to a country like Poland with no more knowledge of Polish to his name than the two Polish words for a "young lady." A foreign correspondent is—or should be— these days something more than a legman, a rewriter of official handouts, a gossip abroad. It is his job and responsibility to mould public opinion; that he cannot do unless he is a scholar, a linguist, a shrewd analyst and motive-prober, and a specialist in his own given area or field.

While the author of this timely book would be the last person to claim that he has all the above qualifications, yet his credentials for the job he undertook in the present volume are many and impressive. He was born of Polish parentage in Milwaukee on July 17, 1911; he attended the parochial school of SS. Cyril & Methodius on Milwaukee's South Side, the heart of Polish Milwaukee; he graduated from the Marquette University High School in 1930 and from the Marquette University College of Journalism in 1934. He served as editor of the suburban weekly *Cudahy Reminder* from 1934 through the first five months of 1935. Since that time he has been police and court reporter for *The Milwaukee Journal*, a wealthy metropolitan daily with a fine journalistic reputation throughout the States. His intimate knowledge of Polish has served him in good stead as a newspaper reporter, and he has covered many outstanding Polish-American events in the United States for his paper.

It is his bilingual knowledge and general background that gives Mr. Kerstein's book its special value. He is no Soviet agent or apologist—like Anna Louise Strong of the Moscow *News* or the Leftist Irving Brant of the Chicago *Sun*, neither with any knowledge of Polish or of the Polish scene and yet posing before the American public as experts on Poland just because they mouth Soviet propaganda as if it were gospel truth. Unlike so many other British and American correspondents stationed in Poland, Mr. Kerstein was never at any time at the mercy of a Soviet-supplied interpreter to "translate," properly colored and trimmed, the reactions of the populace.

This is, in no sense, a reflection upon the ability or integrity of such men in Poland as his fellow-correspondents: Emlyn Williams of *The Christian Science Monitor*, Charles Lambert of *The London Daily Herald*, W. H. Lawrence of *The New York Times*, or Larry Allen of the Associated Press. All these men are trustworthy witnesses and reporters of the chaos that is Poland to-day after the joint Hitler-Stalin invasion and partition of September, 1939, but they are all dependent upon translators and second-hand sources. For instance, at the first press conference of the Soviet-appointed puppet-president for Poland, Bierut (known in the Komintern as Krasnodebski-Rutkowski), for the foreign press, Mr. Kerstein was the sole foreign reporter present who did not need to rely upon the official translations supplied by a young woman who interpreted for the Polish Communist chosen by the Kremlin to head the puppet provisional government of Soviet-dominated Poland.

Mr. Kerstein's vivid dispatches from behind the iron curtain in Poland have been published not only in his own paper, *The Milwaukee Journal*, but have also been syndicated by NANA (North American Newspaper Alliance) and have appeared in such representative American newspapers as the Richmond *News-Leader*, the Toledo *Times*, Cleveland *Plain Dealer*, Springfield (Mass.) *Republican*, Buffalo *News*, Syracuse *Post-Standard*, Louisville *Times*, Cincinnati *Times-Star*, Canton *Repository*, Birmingham *News*, and the Tacoma *News-Tribune*.

Everything that Mr. Kerstein writes in the present volume corroborates and substantiates the report of the Subcommittee No. 2 of the House Committee on Foreign Affairs. This committee, consisting of Representatives Thomas S. Gordon (acting chairman), Joseph F. Ryter, Karl E. Mundt, and Frances P. Bolton, made a European study trip from August 12, 1945, to October 13, 1945, and included Poland in their itinerary. These four deputies of the American people bring back a tragic story (see their private report printed by the U. S. Government for the use of the Committee on Foreign Affairs). More than one succinct paragraph in the above congressional report is amplified and documented by Mr. Kerstein in his comprehensive eye-witness story of Poland under Soviet occupation.

Obtained at considerable personal hazard (the trigger-happy Soviet soldiers in Poland, paid by their generous government all of 15 rubles ($3) a month, are not above supplementing their meagre income in these inflation days with a little banditry on the side, and at night tracer bullets are just as prone to hit a roving American reporter as a hapless Jew who might be expected to have money or valuables on his person), Mr. Kerstein's first-hand story of a Poland still awaiting liberation from Soviet oppression gives one the same authenticity of observation that we have come to expect from a good documentary film. His is a simple, unadorned prose. There is none of that rhetorical overwriting and affected flourishes of style and manner that are so beloved at times of some of our big-time prima donnas of the journalistic circus—star performers on the ideological trapeze who regard themselves as political oracles and pundits as well as ordinary leggers out to report to their everyday readers just what it was they saw and heard in the arenas of their activity. Here are no verbal fireworks to blind the eye and stun the ear but a plain story of terror and betrayal by her allies—at Yalta and at Potsdam—of the first country in Europe to fight Hitler and Nazism at a time when Soviet Russia chose the path of collaboration with the German dictator in a joint campaign of plunder, partition, and annexation of Eastern and Central European states that began in 1939 and continued through June, 1941, when the two partners-in-plunder quarreled—as thieves will—over future booty in the Balkans and in the Middle East (as we now learn from captured enemy documents brought out in the Nuremberg trials).

The aftermath of that infamous pact of the two totalitarian dictators in Europe is unforgettably depicted in these pages that make us all ashamed of the inhumanity of man to man on the approaching eighth anniversary of the Hitler-Stalin partition-and-plunder pact of August 21, 1939, that launched within a few days World War II.

Szymon St. Deptula

Dept. of Polish & Russian
University of Wisconsin

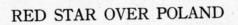

RED STAR OVER POLAND

NICHOLAS COPERNICUS AMID WARSAW'S RUINS

I

CAVES AND CLIFFS

While flying across the Atlantic aboard the Pan-American clipper on September 24, 1945, two United States army majors, who were among the passengers, approached me and inquired where I was going. I explained that I was enroute to central Europe to investigate conditions in Poland.

"Poland!" the majors cried out.

"Are you married?" one of them asked.

"Have you any children?" inquired the other.

When I replied in the affirmative to both questions, the majors shook their heads as though flabbergasted. They stated that they were not envying my mission because they had received reports while they were at their posts in Germany that "a reign of terror prevails in Poland."

"Are you armed?" queried one of the majors, emphasizing that I was on the threshold of a risky mission and a gun might prove quite handy at times in my travels in Poland.

Upon my arrival at Croydon airport, on the outskirts of London, the following day, one of the first persons to engage me in conversation was a Pole employed as a guard in the British immigration office located on the airfield. The Pole stated that he had heard from an immigration officer that I was enroute to Poland.

1

"I have a wife and four children in Lodz, Poland," said the Polish guard, "but I am not returning to Poland. I was advised by an acquaintance who recently fled from Poland that my wife and children do not want me to come back because conditions are so terrible there that they do not want me to return and suffer with them."

On September 26, 1945, I went to the Polish embassy in London to visit the ambassador of the new Polish provisional government to England. The ambassador was not in at the time. The doorman, a Pole in his late fifties, inquired as to why I wanted to see the ambassador. I explained that I had a Polish visa and wanted to discuss my intended mission to Poland with the ambassador. The doorman led me into a small room, closed the door and said in a whispering voice:

"I am a Pole and love Poland very much. But I am never going back to the land of my fathers. People in Poland today are living in fear and hunger, Russian garrisons are stationed everywhere.

"The new Polish provisional government does not represent the people. It represents Russia and receives its orders from Moscow. Thousands of Polish soldiers still stationed in England and Scotland refuse to return to Poland because their country is occupied by the Russians. You are going to Poland and will see for yourself what I tell you is true. I work here in this embassy and know what I am talking about."

The Polish embassy receptionist then explained that he had already applied for an immigration visa to the United States.

"When I get the American visa," he said, "I am going to settle in Chicago, where I plan to live with a brother who is operating a small business."

I obtained flight passage to Warsaw aboard an American Army supply plane in Paris, France, through Alfred H. Lovell, Jr., secretary to Arthur Bliss Lane, American ambassador to Poland. Lovell at the time was staying temporarily at the American embassy in Paris. The supply plane was detained for four hours at the Tempelhof airport in Berlin because the Russians delayed their consent for our flight into Warsaw. Our American Army pilot explained to the small group of embassy employes that the Russians would shoot down our unarmed supply plane if he would make the flight into Warsaw without first procuring Russian consent for the flight.

The supply plane circled over Warsaw four times before landing on the grassy airport, which has no concrete runways. The flying crew explained that they circled the city four times to allow members of the American embassy in the Polish capital sufficient time to drive out to the airport and meet us there. When our plane finally landed, a group of armed Russian soldiers surrounded and eyed us closely. They stood and gaped as the cargo of embassy supplies was being unloaded.

Warsaw from the air was a horrifying picture. Human imagination cannot possibly visualize the hundreds upon hundreds of completely gutted-out buildings. The small group of passengers aboard the supply plane was aghast at the sight of devastated Warsaw, far more ruined than Berlin.

I toured the debris-filled streets of the once proud Polish capital the following few days, noting particularly the many make-shift stands selling innumerable articles and foodstuffs.

Chunks of meat dangled from the boards that make up these stands. The prices of the meat ranged from 60 to 100 zlotys a pound. Bread sold at 15 to 20 zlotys a loaf. Apples sold at 35 zlotys a kilo (about 2¼ pounds). Potatoes sold the cheapest at 4 to 5 zlotys a kilo. Since the Poles in Warsaw earned from 25 to 50 zlotys (25c to 50c) a day, the prices of the foodstuffs were truly exorbitant. Potatoes and bread comprise the principal nourishment of the Poles, for the prices of the other edibles are too steep for their meager earnings.

Scattered throughout Warsaw were the so-called "black markets," where Polish men, women and children sold personal and household articles to procure extra zlotys for necessary food. The Poles hauled out these articles from hiding or salvaged them from the debris of Warsaw. The men and women standing in line sold dresses, flashlights, electric heaters, cameras, neckties, socks, fur coats, shoes, drapes, lamps, electric light bulbs, carpets, chairs, rubber baby nipples and every other conceivable item.

To give you some idea just how these "black markets" in Warsaw looked, imagine a big American department store like Macy's or Gimbels, telling all their store clerks to pick up their merchandise from the counters and walk out on the busiest streets of an American city. Imagine further these clerks shouting to passersby the items they have to sell and the prices. Imagine also thousands of prospective purchasers pushing, jostling, arguing on the streets.

To get the proper background, you would also have to imagine all of the buildings gutted and smashed, for that's the background of these Warsaw "black markets."

These black markets, where you could buy items that you could not even find for sale in America or England because they were not produced during the war, were truly a mockery of life. The ragged, hungry and homeless

Poles were selling expensive cameras, electric flat irons, electric heaters and even luxurious fur coats—for money that would keep body and soul together.

An amazing feature of the black markets was the sale of innumerable American products. For example, a bar of Lux soap was priced at 90 zlotys (90c) and a package of American cigarets at 200 zlotys ($2.00). A can of American packed salmon, shipped to Poland by UNRRA for distribution among the starving Poles, was being sold on the black market at 250 zlotys ($2.50).

Thousands of Poles lived in Warsaw under the most primitive conditions like "cave" and "cliff" dwellers of another era. They had none of the comforts which are taken for granted by Americans in their daily life.

The Polish "cave" dwellers were quartered in basements of buildings smashed to bits by German demolition gangs in revenge for the 1944 insurrection in Warsaw. These "cave" dwellers lived under mounds of debris covering the basements. A hole poked through the debris served as an entrance into the "home." There they made themselves a mattress of straw to sleep on and brought in whatever furniture they were able to salvage from under the rubble of gutted structures. They brought water for their needs from community pumping stations located in various sections of the city.

One old Polish woman in a ragged dress walked in bare feet a quarter of a mile to haul a bucket of water from one of the pumping stations to her home—a small room under a mound of debris that was once her apartment building. This woman did not complain too much. She explained that she was lucky "because other women had to walk more than a mile for a bucket of water."

While the Poles living in these "caves" kept their quarters as clean as possible, they nevertheless are good breeding places for typhus epidemics that periodically break out in Warsaw.

Churches destroyed by the sadistic Germans now held services in basements, the entrances, too, being large holes dug through the mounds of debris. The Poles flocked to these churches even on a week day to pray for their war dead. A sign reading "Wejscie do Kosciola" (Entrance to the Church) was posted above the basement entrance to St. Alexander's Church, completely pulverized by the German Army during the 1944 insurrection. St. Barbara's Church was so devastated that the services were not even held in the basement. Instead, the services were held in the rectory, which served as the church, parish house, office of the diocese and a community auditorium.

Warsaw's "cliff" dwellers occupied the few apartments on the upper floors that were not demolished when the Germans set the buildings afire or threw in hand grenades. One Polish woman lived on the fifth floor of a former six-story apartment building on Ulica Marszalkowska. Her apartment was the only one not destroyed, although the rest of the entire building, with the exception of the steps leading up, was completely gutted.

This freakish apartment consisted of two bedrooms, a living room and bathroom. It was referred to by envious Warsawnians, who lived in caves, as the "eagle's nest."

It was truly a strange sight to observe the motley groups of ragged Poles crawl out of their "caves" or come down from their "cliff" dwellings and swarm down the heaps of debris on their way to work or to the market. One could not help but have the greatest respect and admiration for these people, who in the past six years had been stripped of everything except the wornout clothing on their backs and their courage and energy, besides undergoing the cruel persecution at the hands of the Germans and Russians.

Standing out among the debris-filled streets of Warsaw were scores of shrines dedicated to Poles executed by the Germans. Four crosses painted on a bullet riddled wall designated the spot where 10 Poles had been picked at random on the street and killed by Germans in a drunken stupor. At another shrine, dedicated to four Poles killed by the Germans just to pass their idle time, two boys had stopped on their way home from school. The boys took off their caps and clasped their hands in reverent prayer.

Americans of Polish descent who visited Warsaw before the war broke out in 1939 would be horrified at the heart-breaking damage inflicted on it by the Germans. Only ashes and rubble remain of the once famous, historic capital.

Stare Miasto—(The Old Town)—lies completely in ruins. The Poles for centuries had treasured its character-istic market place, surrounded by buildings of the six-teenth, seventeenth, and eighteenth centuries. Two of them were considered the prettiest: the building No. 27 with a wine shop belonging to the Fukier family and the house No. 32 known as Baryczka's house. The Fukier wine shop, which visitors to Warsaw never failed visiting, dated back to 1590. Baryczka's house was used for years for art exhibitions of the Society for the Preservation of Antiquities. The interior of the Baryczka's house had a very well conserved disposal of rooms, typical of old patrician houses. In the middle of the market place stood a stone statue of a mermaid, which figured in the municipal coat of arms of Warsaw. But all of the famous Stare Miasto, where severe battling between Gen. Tadeusz Bor's insurrectionists against the Germans in 1944 took place, now is a big heap of rubble.

Nothing but rubble likewise remains of the twelfth century St. John's Cathedral, Kolumna Zygmunta, Plac Zamkowy, most beautiful palace of the fifteenth century architecture; Teatr Wielki (Grand Theater), founded by Boguslawski, father of the Polish theater; the city hall, St. Anthony's Church and the Bruhl palace, which housed the Polish foreign office.

Hotel Europejski, the Prudential Life Insurance Co. skyscraper and Pilsudski Square are all big piles of stone and twisted steel. The Germans even desecrated the tomb of Poland's unknown soldier—an act not committed in any other country.

The ghetto was so completely destroyed that not even shells of the buildings remain there, only a big mountain of rubble with grass and weeds already growing wildly over it. Some 150,000 Jews, many of whom hawked their wares in the once busy Nalewki district, were slaughtered there by the Germans.

Some of the Warsaw ghetto homes were three to four stories high, but all were so smashed and completely burned out that hardly a solid brick remains of them. On a warm day the stench of some 30,000 to 50,000 bodies still buried there permeates the air. Thousands of Jews were also dragged out of the ghetto, in addition to the 150,000 killed there, and executed elsewhere by the Germans.

A red blockhouse, which guarded the entrance of the ghetto, stands partly destroyed. During the German occupation, anyone who entered past the gate could be taken for dead because he had no chance of escape. Long walls around the ghetto were topped with sharp, broken glass, which would cut a person into ribbons if he attempted to scale the wall in an effort to escape. Jews in the ghetto were either shot or burned to death. Some Jewish mothers even threw their babies into the fires to prevent prolonged suffering at the hands of the merciless Germans.

The Bank of Poland on Wierzbowa Street was completely wrecked except for part of the first floor, where a large hole in the wall remains mute evidence as to how the Poles in September 1939, dragged out the gold as the German invaders approached. The gold was later transferred safely beyond Poland's borders.

Visible throughout Warsaw are the sewer openings which the Polish insurrectionists entered in their final stand against the Germans. Gen. Bor's Home Army used the sewer system as a means of forwarding communications from general headquarters to the fighters and later to move troops from one section of the city to another. Hundreds of bodies of the insurrectionists were still being removed by reconstruction crews from these sewer passages.

The old American embassy building at 29 Aleje Ujazdowskie is destroyed, and Ambassador Lane had made arrangements to locate a new embassy in a structure two doors away at No. 33, which was less damaged. Ambassador Lane temporarily set up the United States embassy in the Polonia Hotel, which also served as the quarters for other embassies. The Gestapo headquarters at 25 Aleje Szucha, where few Poles ever got out alive once they entered, is now used as the Polish Foreign Office.

The Germans made a special effort to desecrate Polish monuments. For example, they destroyed the Poniatowski statue and shot off the head of the Blessed Virgin at St. Anthony's Church.

The Church of the Holy Cross, built in 1692-1757 and designed by J. Belotti and Anthony Fontanna, was left completely ruined. The heart of the great Polish composer, Frederic Chopin, was immured there. During the German occupation the urn containing Chopin's heart was hidden from the invading Nazis by Bishop Szlagowski in Milanowska. It was returned to Warsaw during a great ceremony on October 17, 1945.

Opposite the Holy Cross Church stood a statue of Nicholas Copernicus, the celebrated Polish astronomer. The statue, cast in bronze from the model by Thorwaldsen in 1830, was stolen by the Germans during the occupation. However, when I was in Warsaw the statue already had been returned and put back in its original setting, with the once splendid buildings around it in total ruins.

American troops found the statue of Copernicus and efforts were made to immediately return it to Poland following the collapse of Germany. The Poles related this interesting sidelight regarding the statue:

"Copernicus held in his hand a metal globe. When the Germans were removing the statue, the globe fell out of Copernicus' hand and rolled onto the pavement. Later, when the statue was returned, a new globe was made to fit Copernicus' hand, but suddenly a Pole showed up with the original globe, stating that he had picked it up when the Germans hurried away the statue. The Pole said that he was confident that Copernicus would return to Poland, for he belonged to Poland and not to Germany as the Germans had claimed, and for that reason he had hidden the original globe."

Despite the wanton German destruction of Warsaw, Ulica Marszalkowska—Warsaw's Broadway—congested with vehicular and pedestrian traffic, remains the devastated capital's busiest street. Likewise, the popular Maly Teatr (The Little Theater), seating 200, plays to a full house each day. Oddly enough, the movie that attracted the Poles to the Maly Teatr in the fall of 1945 was entitled "Warsaw Under Occupation."

Following the defeat and departure of the German Army, Polish pioneer cleanup brigades cleared Warsaw's grounds from more than 200,000 unexploded mines. The work was so thorough that only a few mines remain for cleanup. Occasionally, shells of buildings collapse and fall into the streets especially when the winds are strong.

Warsaw's reconstruction office issued lengthy statements about the future reconstruction of the Polish capital, but nothing was being done on a large scale to remove the debris and to raze the ghostlike structures. There is a noticeable lack of bulldozers, razing cranes with heavy iron balls that smash gutted buildings and other reconstruction equipment so common in America. Poles stand hazardously on tall walls of gutted structures prying out bricks with crowbars or smashing the weakened masonry with sledge hammers—a slow, tedious and dangerous process.

While Warsaw was battered to bits by the Germans in a matter of a few weeks during the 1944 insurrection, it will take the Poles generations to rebuild it.

II

JANIE

Polish children, like their elders, suffered greatly under the German occupation, for the Germans displayed no consideration to the youngsters. Take Joasia (Janie), 11 year old daughter of Edward G. Piotrowski, who was employed as a translator for United States Ambassador Lane. She was only 5 years old when the German Blitzkrieg hit Poland on September 1, 1939. Her father gave me a copy of a letter which she had written to her brother, Andrew, a Polish Air Corps lieutenant still in western Europe. The letter was written late in September, 1945, shortly after Gen. Eisenhower's visit to Warsaw.

"This letter will explain better than I can the sufferings of the children of Poland during the German occupation because it was written by a Polish child and contains her impressions presented in her own individual style," said Mr. Piotrowski.

Janie was a pretty girl with braided pigtails, their ends tied with shredded, tiny red ribbons. She wore a weatherbeaten red tam and badly worn plaid coat, darned tan stockings and scuffed black shoes. The Piotrowskis, like so many other Warsaw people, live in a bombed apartment. Their address is 6 Ulica Senatorska.

Mr. Piotrowski was showing me Janie's letter to Andrew when she suddenly walked into his office at the American embassy.

12

"Did you stand Vigil on Ulica Piusa XI?" Mr. Piotrowski asked his daughter.

"Yes, father, for a whole hour," replied Joasia. "We prayed and cried. We could not help crying, father."

Janie's hour-long vigil was at Warsaw's most hallowed shrine on Ulica Piusa XI, where 100 Poles were shot on October 17, 1944, by the Germans because the Warsaw Poles had knocked out a German tank loaded with Polish women on the front as "protection" against the insurrectionists' antitank shells. The Poles threw gasoline bottles and ignited them to knock out the tank, thus sparing the women from death. The Germans became so irate that they picked 100 Polish men off the streets, stood them against the wall of a building and shot them. The shrine, consisting of a statue of the Blessed Virgin, candles and a vase of flowers, is on a bullet-riddled wall of a gutted-out four-story building. The knocked-out German tank still stands in the street at the shrine.

Janie's letter to her brother follows:

"Dear Andrew: I do not remember you any more because I was a very little girl when you left Warsaw, but mother and father told me a lot about you and about Grazynka, and I know from Aunty Musia that far away I have a grown-up brother and sister. I'm proud of you because you have been fighting Germans and riding in airplanes. I hate the Germans very much because they have done us so much wrong.

"During the insurrection we stayed for four months in a cellar without light or water. We ate mouldy dried bread. I still had some chocolate and sardines from you, and then we had to come out to the Germans because we were very hungry and weak. We did not care any more whether they would shoot us or whether we would die in the cellar. So they then took us to a camp and were going to shoot us.

"Already they had put us up to a wall, with Wojciech and Nadzia and Stanislaw and his family, but somehow at the last moment they changed their minds. I was not afraid at all, only I prayed to dear God that they might shoot me first, so I would not look on as they were shooting mother and father. And I hate them because they killed dear Nunusia, running her over with an automobile. That was dreadful. I cried for a long time and didn't want to have another little dog any more. But now I would like to have one very much, only mother has no money to buy me a little Pekinese. The doll I received from you was all the time with me in the cellar. And then the Germans trod on her and crushed her, when they were taking our things away.

"I like Americans very much. I have been with father to see Mrs. Ambassador, such a beautiful lady. Father brings me lots of chocolate and chewing gum. Do you like chewing gum? If you do, I shall keep it for you.

"P. S.—Yesterday, Gen. Eisenhower came to Warsaw by airplane and shook hands with father. Father said he was your chief commander. I'm sorry I could not see him or his airplane, so I asked father to ask him about you."

Janie's Warsaw, the capital of Poland, prior to Sept. 1, 1939, when Germany's war machine began to crush her smaller Polish neighbor, was truly a continental metropolis—with splendid theaters, concert halls, an imposing opera house, many fine churches, schools, parks, monuments, a modern "grand central" railroad station, an up-to-date airport, night clubs, cafes and many other metropolitan features.

Her brilliant, gay, tolerant and hospitable Warsaw of 1939 had a setting so magnificent on the banks of the Vistula that it enchanted the visitor. As Polish cities go, Warsaw is comparatively young, having been the capital only 400 years, but despite its "youth" it did have its age-old castles and palaces, its Stare Miasto (Old City)— a square bordered by the bright colored town houses and carved doorways of former merchant princes and the nobility of another age. Most visitors took in Stare Miasto to sample Poland's incomparable cuisines and to sip of the world's oldest wines at Fukier's wine shop, opened just before the Pilgrims landed at Plymouth.

Moreover, in 1939 there still stood the old castle (zamek) of the Polish kings with richly decorated rooms dating from the thirteenth century and the beautiful Lazienki palace of the last Polish ruler, King Stanislaw August Poniatowski, dating from the end of the seventeenth century, with period furniture. On the outskirts were chiefly the fine villas built after the first World War, when Poland was resurrected as a free nation following the three partitions in 1772, 1793 and 1795, in which Russia, Germany and Austria participated.

Today, all of proud Warsaw's splendor and gaiety are gone, for Warsaw lies in hideous ruins, having been demolished in the most systematic manner imaginable by ruthless German soldiers in revenge for the 1944 insurrection.

The Poles today are singing a song that reflects their sadness over the ruins of their once proud, beautiful capital and their dynamic will to rebuild it. The song, entitled "A Song About My Warsaw," is the No. 1 hit tune of postwar Poland. The words and music were composed by Albert Harris, a young man of Lodz, Poland, while he was in Russian captivity.

The melody and words are heartbreaking in parts and stirring toward the end. Harris successfully caught the Poles' feelings regarding Warsaw's ruins and vividly expressed it in this popular song, which has also scored a hit with the Americans stationed at the embassy. Nobody dances when the song is sung or played. It is not that kind of a song.

Mieczyslaw Fogg, who appeared on many stages in America before the second World War, sings the song to great acclaim in Warsaw. He now operates a cafe amid the ruins of the Polish capital.

To fully appreciate "A Song About My Warsaw," a person would have to hear the melody and the song sung in Polish. The following translation will, however, give some idea of it to American readers:

> As the smile of the girl whom you love,
> As the bursting of spring all anew,
> As the flight of the red footed dove,
> The smell of fresh grass all adew,
> As the love of youth's heart all alight,
> As the song of the nightingale bright,
> So my heart does rejoice at this sweet melody
> That Warsaw is always to me!

*   *   *

> Oh, Warsaw, beloved, dear Warsaw!
> I dream of you night and day
> I dream of your fully thronged streets
> I dream of your gaily decked highways.
> I know that you're calling to me,

So longing until you are free
How deeply I long to retain you again,
Oh, Warsaw, I dream of your fame!

* * *

How I long to retrace my own steps,
The steps of my long flown youth.
The streets all alit by the moon,
Let's stroll down the old avenue,
Let's gaze at the Vistula again,
And wait for a train all in vain,
And see you rejoicing and laughing once more!
Oh, Warsaw, beloved, dear Warsaw!

* * *

I know that you're not now the same,
That dark blood has washed all your streets.
I'm proud that you know no shame,
Though now you have caused me to weep.
And now though you're low in the mud,
I'll rebuild with my own sweat and blood,
So Warsaw shall rise once again to her might,
I swear on my heart and life.

A Pail of Water

III

POLAND AFTER HITLER

The Polish provisional government, strictly a Russian puppet government, found the ruins of Warsaw an ideal setting in which to set up its headquarters in the Soviet drive to communize the war weary, hungry, ragged, homeless Poles. However, as during the German occupation, the Poles proved unwilling in accepting a form of government or a foreign ideology in which they have neither voice nor freedom. That explains why even though the war in Europe had officially ended months ago, gunfire was frequently heard in war-scarred Poland in the fall of 1945 and dead bodies littered streets and highways especially in the morning.

Living conditions throughout the Polish hinterland did not improve with the defeat and departure of the merciless German invaders. The Polish nation remained a war ravaged, unhappy country without political freedom, without freedom of press, without freedom of assembly and even without freedom of speech. The Russian hammer and sickle replaced the German swastika. Portraits of Stalin replaced those of Hitler. Russian soldiers and the dreaded NKVD (Russian secret police) took the place of German soldiers and the cruel Gestapo gangsters in uniform and civilian clothes. Efforts were in full progress to propagandize each Pole with Communism instead of

Nazism as the Germans unsuccessfully tried to do throughout their almost six years of occupation.

The Polish government-controlled newspapers in their editorials bitterly assailed foreign correspondents for writing about the shootings and robberies, but those are undisputable facts. The shootings, robberies and beatings were even reported in the very same Polish newspapers that editorially attacked the foreign correspondents for their "untruthful articles" about the shootings.

For example, the governmental newspaper *Zycie Warszawy* (Warsaw Life) in its October 5, 1945, edition carried this item:

"The factory committee for the reconstruction of the Poniatowski bridge in Warsaw raised a protest in connection with the wounding of one of their workers by a shot fired by a militiaman on the pontoon bridge on October 1 (1945) at 7:10 a.m. The worker was going to work in company with other workers. No warning was given. These cases of shootings are getting more and more frequent and were even discussed at the session of the Warsaw national council. Such shootings and this way of carrying on must stop."

And on October 19, 1945, the same governmental newspaper stated:

"The safety of railroad transport requires radical action. According to accounts arriving from the country district, railway transportation takes place in conditions which remind one of the jungle, desert areas filled with gangs of robbers, with no police or military protection. Small convoys, placed there by private institutions, cannot do much in these cases. Coal transports are sometimes robbed of up to 20% to 30% of their contents. Sometimes whole carloads disappear. Other articles are also stolen.

First of all, the railway guards should be sifted; secondly, the trains should run more directly and not stop at every station. Cars should not be detached on the way, as in such a manner some of them simply 'disappear.' The escorts must be strengthened greatly, going as far as military convoying in case of need."

The same newspaper in its October 31, 1945, issue reported as follows:

"CRIME IN ZYRARDOW! On the 27th the manager of the Zyrardow tannery, Joseph Matuszewski, was mortally wounded by a number of shots fired by criminal hands, as he got out of his car. He was a former member of the AK (Polish underground army active against Hitler throughout the war but now frowned upon by the Bierut puppet government), and became secretary of the Democratic party in Zyrardow. He has been manager of the tannery since May 1."

A high Polish law enforcement officer—equivalent to chief of police in a metropolitan American city—in the new area of Poland stated that everyone in his country was afraid to talk and move around. He added that people are shot by the Russians at all hours of the day and night, with the black market being the most familiar "shooting scene."

He said that government officials are watching each other for fear that some of them may be members of the secret police. He explained that he had already shot in a single night as many as 15 Russian soldiers and army deserters caught looting, robbing and attacking Poles. He said, "I drive around in a car among the ruins and shoot the Russians right in the head when I catch them molesting Poles."

This law enforcement officer stated that he was so disgusted with conditions in Poland that he planned on leaving his country time and again.

"Each time, however, I change my mind and stay because I feel someone who has the courage to prevent the Russians from robbing and killing the Poles must stay," he said. "If I wanted to escape from Poland, I have a splendid means of doing so in my capacity as an official. But I feel that my duty is to remain in my fatherland and face the hardships that we Poles all are undergoing."

While Bierut's government was boasting about the "German industrial areas" annexed to western Poland, many Poles complained that such annexations are "only seeds for a future war when Germany again rises on its feet."

"We are not benefiting at all from the annexation of the German industrial Silesian territories because the Russians are stripping the industrial plants and ports of all machinery," a Polish citizen in the new area said. "Furthermore, the homes and buildings in the former German towns and cities are terribly battered and will take generations to rebuild. Besides, when the Germans ever get back on their feet they will demand the return of their lost territories from Poland. Thus, I and many other Poles in my community here look upon the annexation of the German territories to Poland as tantamount to seeds for a future war."

A number of Poles are mourning the loss of the 70,000 square miles of eastern Poland to Russia. Some 5,000,000 Poles who lived in that area are being moved westward into Poland, particularly into the territories that formerly were German. The Poles complaining about the loss of the eastern Polish territory are especially mournful over the loss of Lwow and Wilno, which they claim are truly Polish in character and flavor.

Lwow, with a population of 250,000, was the largest city in "Eastern Little Poland." It is situated amongst the Roztocze hills, the highest known as the "Gora Zamkowa" (Castle Mountain) and topped with a mount commemorating the union of Lublin between Poland and Lithuania in 1569.

Wilno, a city of some 200,000 inhabitants, was the cultural, political and economic center of Northeastern Poland. On the market place stood the university, which was founded in 1578 by King Stefan Batory. The neighborhood of Wilno is rich in lakes.

The government press sensed the complaints of Poles regarding the annexation of the former German territories. For example, the *Glos Ludu* (Communist "Voice of the People") in its October 9, 1945, edition, stated:

"International reaction is watching how the western lands are used by Polish democracy, in order, if possible to deny Poland the age-old right to these lands. The western lands need to be provisioned from the poor central provinces. That is why reaction is agitating so strongly against the delivery in kind of food by the peasants. But the Polish peasant will not be fooled and will do his duty."

The government-controlled press is also constantly agitating against the formation of new political parties on the grounds that "it is harmful to make more parties, for this may cause breaks." At a meeting of the Communist Polish Workers' party and the Polish Socialist party, held in Lublin in the latter part of October, 1945, the collaborating "left wingers" stressed Poland's alliance with Russia, and the cooperation of both parties as being the most numerous parties on which the Polish government bases itself." The speakers further emphasized:

"It is harmful to form more parties, for this may cause breaks. The main problem of economic policy is maintaining in the hands of the government large industry, foreign trade, power-production and communication. The government is favorable to the peasants, taking 'only 25%' of their crops as the contingents. The peasants may dispose freely of the rest. The situation of the municipal population is worse, as it cannot purchase a sufficient amount of foodstuffs at stiff prices. A raise in salaries would not solve the situation, but would bring about inflation."

My investigation disclosed a soul-chilling wave of antagonism in Poland—a bitter atmosphere of resentment against the "despotic decrees" of Bierut's marionette government sponsored by Russia, against the strongly entrenched Russian garrisons and against the current living conditions.

This dissatisfaction was reaching a boiling point in the ruins of Warsaw, in the impoverished villages, in the German areas annexed to Poland, in any part of Poland you visit. The Polish security or secret police are functioning day and night to stem the tide of antagonism, arresting the bitterest and loudest critics of the puppet government.

Government officials, while speaking highly about the spirit of cooperation among the Polish people, were fully cognizant of the dissatisfaction that prevails.

To counteract any dissatisfaction, Bierut issued a decree establishing courts-martial for all crimes against "public safety, public order of the economic interests of the state." Under this decree, the accused Poles have no right of appealing their sentences, which are carried out in 24 hours and range from one year in prison to death.

Many of the Poles with whom I have spoken looked around cautiously before engaging me in a conversation, for fear that someone—a security policeman—might be listening.

The terror under which the Poles are living in the newly annexed area was described to me in detail by a young attractive widow, about 25 years old. She stated that her husband, a Polish pilot, was killed at Katyn by the Russians. She added that her father was also killed by the Russians in Warsaw.

"I lived throughout the insurrection of 1944 in Warsaw and headed a group of girls making hand grenades that were hurled against the Germans," she told me. "I know more about making hand grenades than most soldiers. My storm battalion was composed of girls 15 to 20 years old.

"You should have seen those 15- and 16-year-old girls fight. They did not fear shell fire or bombs. While making their hand grenades, these girls would sing touching songs expressing hopes for a new free Poland. Nothing has hurt any of us as much as the burning and dynamiting of our beautiful Warsaw. Warsaw to us Poles was really Poland."

This young widow then went on to discuss her present life. She told me that her greatest wish was that I report back to America, especially to the American women, what she had to say about present life in postwar Poland. There were no tears in her eyes as she related her story:

"After six years of hell, I as a woman certainly feel entitled to the freedom and gayety of life, but instead hellish conditions still continue around me in Poland.

This is Sunday night. In America the women are out enjoying themselves at theaters, dance halls and other places of amusement, while I pace the floors of my home, afraid to venture outside.

"It is not safe being outdoors because the Russians molest all Polish women. That is why I and the other Polish women confine ourselves to our homes. On one occasion a Russian soldier struck me in the cheek and broke two of my teeth when I went outside. On another occasion a Russian soldier grabbed me by the arm and twisted it so badly that he almost broke it. I grappled with him and finally got away.

"No foreigners can understand the miserable life of a Pole. The war is over everywhere except here in Poland. Poles are being shot by the Russians at the rate of 50 a week in this city and there is no redress for the killers. I saw two Poles shot by the Russians in front of my home. On several occasions the Russians have even entered this home and stolen articles they wanted. I hope that you tell the truth about the real conditions in Poland. Let the world know what hell on earth the Poles still have after six years of war against the Germans.

"I don't mind telling you the truth because I don't care what happens to me. I may be shot soon anyway. No Pole in Poland has any peace, unless he is buried. The Russians do not want any Poles alive. They want to finish us all."

"The biggest mistake," the Polish widow went on to say, "now being made is the repatriation of the Poles from western Europe. The Poles would be better off remaining where they are for at least there they would remain alive. When the Poles come here they are practically signing a death warrant. Many of those who return come to me daily and with tears in their eyes ask me to help them return to the British displaced-persons camps in Germany. They explain to me that they had been robbed by the Russians, either in their newly settled homes or on trains en route to the places where they were to settle."

An interesting sidelight in the Polish widow's life during the war against Germany was the fact that in Warsaw she provided a refuge for two British airmen who had been shot down by the Germans. The British airmen lived in her home for six weeks after fleeing from a Polish concentration camp. She and other Poles successfully planned an escape of these two Englishmen out of Poland.

Similar complaints about present conditions in Poland were echoed by other Polish women. In one village a woman stated:

"All those who want to stay in the new Polish areas must join the Communist PPR (Polish Workers' Party); otherwise they will be thrown out."

In Poznan a housewife said that conditions were "very hard."

"There is scarcely any pay," she said, "and food prices are exorbitant. So everyone trades anything he has. But now even that is coming to a stop. Taxes are terrible. Electric current, instead of 20 groszy (one-fifth of a zloty) as under German occupation, now costs three zlotys a kilowatt. The same with gas.

"Apartment rents have risen 100 to 200%. For war damage one has to contribute 100 to 200 zlotys ($1 to $2) monthly and my husband earns only 1,000 zlotys ($10) a month.

"Out of what America sent through UNRRA, we once got some canned meat, one half kilogram (about 1⅛ pounds) of lard and a kilogram (about 2¼ pounds) of dried prunes. We have ration cards, but they do not give anything on them except occasionally tasteless black bread. We have come from bad to worse. This must change because we will not stand it."

This housewife complained also that the price of bread had doubled—from 20 zlotys (20c) a loaf to 40 zlotys. This price increase was made at the time when the government newspaper *Zycie Warszawy* stated editorially: "Recently, we have brought about with satisfaction a slow but steady lowering of the prices of various foodstuffs."

One woman in the new Polish territory said that her monthly wages were sufficient only for a week's maintenance. Asked about rations, she explained that she gets a bit of sugar, fat and black bread each month.

"You surely are fortunate," she asserted. "You can go back to America, but we Poles must stay here and suffer."

I also interviewed a number of Polish businessmen in the new areas regarding postwar conditions in Poland. I asked one of them whether under these dreadful conditions, which he had related to me, settlers in the new Polish area did not simply give up and return where they had come from. This businessman replied:

"Conditions in other parts of Poland also are far from satisfactory. Many settlers had come from Krakow, Warsaw, Poznan and Lublin in the hope of finding better opportunities and atmosphere."

He said that "economic and business conditions are virtually hopeless here." He described the administration for the government's reconstruction program as "being without a head and without feet, and therefore it could have no backbone." He stated that the "officials for the most part were of a very inferior caliber." As far as the militia, which serves as a police force is concerned, "the members are recruited chiefly from the riffraff," he said.

Asked whether there was fear of secret police in his community, the businessman stated emphatically, "Indeed there is considerable fear of secret police. Nobody is safe from arrest. Nobody has freedom and security."

Then asked about conditions in other parts of Poland —that is, from the point of personal liberty—he stated that dreadful things occurred in the eastern part of the country.

"In Lublin periodic visits are made to homes by the secret police," he said. "Members of the underground army are being executed regularly in groups."

In a book store that I entered with Foreign Correspondents Emlyn Williams and Charles Lambert, we noticed one large section of a book counter covered with a huge Polish map.

I picked up this map and under it I saw hundreds of communistic pamphlets in the Polish language. The covers of these pamphlets were printed in red ink. Some of these pamphlets were authored by Molotov and other Communist leaders of Russia. The bookstore proprietor explained to us that the Polish provisional government had forced these pamphlets on him, but that he covered them up with a map because he does not believe in Communism, as do neither most of his customers. He said that when he notices a secret police agent entering the store he quickly moves the map to the other section of the counter and thus exhibits the communistic pamphlets "for my own protection against arrest."

In this same city I entered a stationery and religious goods store with Williams and Lambert. In the store we noted two empty showcases, and I asked the woman operator about them. She led Williams, Lambert and me to the rear of the store.

Pointing to a broken window, she explained that a group of Russian soldiers the night before had broken in and stolen all of the woolen goods and religious articles that were in the two showcases. We asked her how she knew that Russian soldiers had entered her store. She explained that these Russian soldiers had been in a tavern-restaurant prior to the burglary. Upon becoming drunk there, she said, the Russians went into the kitchen and stole a quantity of sausage, chewed on it, spat some of it back on the floor and then threw other sausages against the walls. They then left the tavern-restaurant and its proprietor watched them break into the stationery and religious goods store next door.

While this woman was relating the details of the burglary to us, a man suddenly dashed into the store, cried out excitedly, "I cannot see you now. The Russians have just broken into my home and robbed it," and rushed out. The remarks were addressed to a male clerk who had been awaiting the man.

A Polish Army lieutenant came to my hotel room in Krakow and with tears in his eyes said: "Please take me to America with you. I will be your valet and keep your suit neatly pressed and your shoes polished. I'll do all the scrubbing in your home. I will be your lifelong faithful servant. I will do anything for you if you will only get me out of Poland."

I told him that his duty was to stay in Poland, his country and rebuild it in the American pattern since he was fond of America.

"That's the trouble," he told me. "I know my duty is to remain here and rebuild my country but the Russians are constantly interfering with the Polish soldiers. All my superior officers are Russians who can't even read Polish maps. All the orders regarding our army and government come from Moscow. We are not free. We are under Russian occupation."

The lieutenant, who took part in many battles and was wounded twice, sobbed as he talked to me. "Maybe you think I'm soft," he said, "but I am not. I have been in many battles."

He stated that he had been asked time and again by his superior Russian officer to join the Communist Polish Workers party, but he had refused to do so.

"I am a Pole," said the soldier. "I could not join the Communist party because I am opposed to it in heart and mind. Look at my boots and uniform. They are old and worn out. I am a lieutenant in the Polish Army, but I do not even have a pistol. I was told that if I join the Polish Workers party, I would get new boots, a new uniform and a pistol. As much as I want and need all those things, I cannot in conscience join the party and sell out my country to the Russians."

An American GI who shared my hotel room was moved when I translated the Polish lieutenant's story as it progressed. The GI, who had a Purple Heart for wounds suffered in Germany, remarked to me: "To think that I had been fighting to free Poland and other small nations only to see something like this happen."

The lieutenant walked up to the GI and closely examined the GI's uniform, praised it and then requested whether he could examine the GI's revolver. The GI handed him the revolver.

"Colt .45," beamed the Pole.

Throughout my travels in Poland I was advised that all the higher officers in the Polish Army were Russians dressed in Polish Army uniforms, many of whom could not even speak or understand a word of Polish. For example, at a dinner that I attended I saw a Polish Army colonel bedecked with medals—one the Virtuti Militari, highest Polish military honor, and a sparkling medal with a picture of Stalin. I approached the colonel and spoke to him in Polish. I got no response. I was told by another guest at the dinner that the "Polish Army colonel" was a Russian who does not speak Polish.

I have also had experience with the Polish secret police. One of the secret policemen escorted me on a tour of a newly acquired Polish city, advising me not to listen to the complaints of the Poles about their grievances involving Russian soldiers "because the Poles do not appreciate that Poland would not be free today if it were not for Russia." He urged me to write about the German atrocities. This secret agent entered the homes of Poles at any time of day or night. He frequently entered the homes of Polish families who were my hosts in Szczecin. I was advised by my hosts to refrain from talking freely while he was in our midst "because we may be arrested after your departure." This agent had introduced himself to me as "Mr. Lewandowski" and told me he was related to "a prominent man movie star in Hollywood."

Poland's typhoid fever rate was increasing at the rate of 2,000 cases per week in October. In addition, there were some 1,000,000 cases of venereal disease, and the tuberculosis rate was extremely high. While UNRRA has shipped tons of DDT and vaccines to prevent epidemics, many Poles stated that none of these preventives were being distributed on any noticeable scale. A number of UNRRA workers from foreign countries confidentially stated that they were disgusted with the distribution of UNRRA articles turned over to the Polish government ministries for distribution.

One American embassy woman said that while she was eating one night in the Polonia hotel dining room a Russian soldier grabbed her by the arm and insisted on dancing with her. She refused. A commotion followed. She finally loosed her arm from the grasp of the Russian and fled in tears and terror to her hotel room.

An American embassy car was halted on the highway and the American Army officer who was driving was compelled to surrender his tire jack and pump on orders of a Russian Army colonel or "lose" the car.

One day another correspondent, an American soldier, a guide and I went to view the Gen. Thaddeus Kosciuszko mound outside of Krakow. Five Russian soldiers suddenly appeared and vigorously objected to our taking pictures. One of the Russian officers demanded that we surrender the cameras, but after some 20 minutes of explaining, during which our guide told the Russians that Kosciuszko helped the Americans win the Revolutionary War and meant much to them in history, the Russians settled the affair by confiscating our films and allowing us to keep the cameras.

I have seen a Russian Army convoy of trucks stop at homes of newly settled Poles in the Oder area and the Russian soldiers enter the homes and come out with lamps, radios, tables, chairs and other articles despite the strenuous objections of the owners.

While I was in Krakow, an aged Polish woman requested assistance in locating her husband.

"My husband and 400 other Polish men were taken away from here by the Russian Army," she wept. "I have never heard from him since. You are an American. Perhaps you can help me locate him."

The average Pole believes in strong, friendly relations with Russia, but he deplores having his country occupied by Russian troops and ruled by a Soviet-sponsored government in which he neither has a voice nor representation.

"We do not have a democracy here at all in Poland," said a Pole in Warsaw. "We have a despotic form of government.

"Our government officials have not been chosen by the people. Instead, they were hand picked by the Russians in Moscow.

"We Poles want to be friends with Russia, but we don't want to be ruled by her. We want our own government of the people, by the people and for the people. We want to have our own voice in making our own laws. We do not want to be ruled as we are now by the decrees of the Bierut government. We in Poland want to live as free people like you Americans in the United States."

While the Bierut government in the fall of 1945 was publicizing the vast land reform program, I heard the peasants complaining about the small land allotments given them and about the "delivery in kind" taxes levied on them. For example, one peasant said that the government had levied on his farm a delivery in kind (farm produce) tax so high that his own crops would not be enough.

"I would have to give everything," he explained, "and buy some more. I must deliver up 25 kilograms of butter, 30 kilograms of cheese, 120 eggs, some 200 kilograms of grain and potatoes. I may have to give up a cow if I don't meet the levy."

Under the land reform program, many peasants complained that they received as little as two or three hectares of land. One of them receiving such a bit of land said, "Even this small piece of land is of no value to me because I am without farm tools and implements, livestock, fertilizer, seeds and barns."

Such was the lot of thousands of Polish peasants in the fall of 1945.

Organized political action cannot be developed in Poland without permission from the administrative authorities of the Polish puppet government.

"This proves beyond a doubt that Poland is not a democracy," one political leader in pre-war Poland stated in the study of his home. "The provisional government understands only as 'democracy' what it believes to be democracy, regardless of the will of the majority of the people. It is for that reason that the provisional government does not respect freedom of the press and assembly."

When I asked this veteran political leader of pre-war Poland what he understood "democracy" to mean, he answered:

"A democracy is a government operated by the people, for the people and through the representatives of the people chosen in free elections. A democracy is a government such as exists in the United States."

One day Lt. William J. Tonesk, naval attache to the United States embassy in Warsaw, and I dined with a Polish Army colonel, who was just divested of his rank and returning to civilian life after having participated in many battles against the Germans. This ex-colonel, wearing his uniform bedecked with medals for the last time, explained that he had $500 in American money buried in the ground for many years.

"I am going to apply for an immigration visa to the United States," said the Polish ex-colonel. "When I am granted such a visa, I am going to dig out the $500 and leave Poland to settle in America. There is no freedom here in Poland. The people have no voice in their government. I am being demobilized and my rank of colonel is being taken away from me against my will after fighting for Poland's freedom six long years against the Germans. My country now is occupied by the Russians and we have no real Polish Army, since all the high ranking officers in the so-called Polish Army are Russians."

The Polish ex-colonel wiped his tears with an old handkerchief as he spoke about the misery and lack of freedom in Poland.

A Polish youth, about 20 years old, likewise complained about the lack of freedom in his country. He said that he had great difficulty in enrolling as an architectural student at the University of Krakow because he did not belong to the Communist Polish Workers' party.

"I am going to leave Poland and settle somewhere on a South Sea island in the Pacific when I get the opportunity to do so," said the Polish youth. "I want to live free like you Americans."

Thus it was throughout my travels in the Polish hinterland in the fall of 1945. Pole after Pole—men as well as women—spoke about the lack of freedom and democracy in Poland. They complained about their puppet government set up by Russia and catering only to Russia, about the plundering Russian garrisons, the dreaded NKVD and the absolute lack of law and order. Pole after Pole expressed a desire to leave Poland and settle in a truly democratic haven, where people are ruled by a government of the people, by the people and for the people.

The lack of freedom in Poland explains why 284,000 Poles in displaced persons' camps in western Europe have repeatedly refused to return home. Many of them are living under difficult conditions behind fences in preference to repatriation to their native land, where they would return willingly under another government chosen by the majority of the Poles in free and unfettered elections, not the type of rigged elections held in Poland on Sunday, January 19, 1947. The United States Army has forbidden forcible repatriation of Poles from its zone in Germany, except in cases involving wanted war criminals.

Charles Rozmarek, Chicago, president of the Polish American Congress, has proposed to the United States government that America should take the lead in providing new homes, where the displaced Poles could earn their daily bread, instead of providing billions of dollars for maintaining them in idleness in Germany. Rozmarek, who has made a thorough study of the German camps, charged that "many displaced Poles are being moved from camp to camp in Germany in an effort to force them against their will to return to Poland."

IV

HOW RUSSIA GOT POLAND INTO HER CLUTCHES

Soviet Russia established the puppet Polish provisional government in Moscow even before the defeat of Germany.

Through a constant barrage of propaganda Russia insinuated that the London Polish government in exile was following the Nazi pattern and favored only the large Polish landowners. This propaganda emanated from Moscow throughout the war despite the fact that the London Polish government was bitterly opposed to Nazism and directed the Polish underground army of Gen. Bor in continuing acts of sabotage against the German Army and in constantly disrupting the German lines of communication during the occupation.

The object of this propaganda was to confuse the Polish government issue and thereby lay the groundwork for a Russian-sponsored government. The first step toward this direction was taken early in 1943 when Soviet Russia broke off relations with the London Polish government, charging it was following the Nazi propaganda line. Another strategic move was made in January, 1945, when the Russian-sponsored Polish Committee for National Liberation proclaimed itself the government of Poland, and Russia announced immediately that it was giving this committee its recognition.

Russia's objective was achieved at the Yalta Conference early in 1945. Agreement was reached on a formula to solve the government problem in Poland. The formula provided that a new government, composed of "democratic elements from within Poland and abroad," was to be formed, and when the government gave promises of "free and unfettered elections" it was to win recognition of Great Britain and America.

Following this agreement on a new government, the Warsaw cabinet, chosen by Soviet Russia, early in July, 1945, informed America and Britain that free elections by secret ballot would be held "as soon as conditions permit." In Washington, President Truman issued the text of the message he sent to Edward Osobka-Morawski, Polish prime minister. It read in part, "The government of the United States . . . on the basis of its assurance at the Crimea Conference, hereby establishes relations with the Polish Provisional Government of National Unity."

Secretary of State James F. Byrnes, in his first official diplomatic communication after taking office, telegraphed Foreign Minister Wincenty Rzymowski: "I trust that these relations may forever remain cordial and friendly."

From London similar messages were sent by the British to Warsaw and the Polish government problem was officially settled to the utmost satisfaction of Soviet Russia.

Since no date was set for the "free and unfettered elections," the Russian-sponsored Polish provisional government was given plenty of leeway and time to pattern the Polish country until it felt that the time was "ripe" for it to win an election. Huge Russian Army garrisons and innumerable NKVD (Russian secret police) units were stationed throughout Poland to assist the

Communist government leaders in enforcing the Moscow-dictated decrees and in taking out of circulation the Poles heard voicing opinions against such decrees. The methods used were similar to those utilized by the Bolsheviks in seizing the government in Russia and in maintaining it. Mass arrests of Communist critics became as frequent in Poland as they were in Russia when the Bolsheviks first seized the control of government in Russia.

Russia entrusted the presidency of the Polish provisional government to mild-mannered Boleslaw Bierut, but the real power to rule and to shape Poland along communistic lines was placed in the hands of dynamic Wladyslaw Gomolka, vice-premier and the leader of the Polish Workers' party, which is the camouflaged Communist party in Poland.

Fifty-six-year-old Bierut is of medium stature. He sports a short mustache, wears dark-rimmed glasses. He wore a dark gray suit on the night of his first presidential press conference which I attended in Belvedere Palace in Warsaw. Bierut lived in the palace, closely guarded by Polish soldiers armed with machine guns.

Bierut spoke at great length about the relationship between Poland and Russia, emphasizing that "many foreigners seeing this process of democratization in Poland think that this is being influenced by Russia and the Red Army."

"Such a point of view is often set out in the foreign press," said Bierut, "but it is not the real explanation. The Polish people for a long time understood what its former government did not understand. And that is that the Polish people must live in neighborly manner with its Russian neighbor.

"Now that the Polish nation has been liberated—thanks to the Red Army—the Polish people realize even more than ever before that the German danger will always exist. Poland, akin to other Slavic nations, feels the need of cultural relations with the Soviet Union. Peace in Europe depends on the friendly relations in eastern Europe between Poland and Soviet Russia."

Bierut emphasized that "if these relations are friendly, the future of Poland and its neighbor will be great and easy." He stated that "Poland had signed an agreement with Soviet Russia for 25 years."

"The agreement settles Poland's questions with her Soviet neighbor," he explained. "Similar agreements will be made with all our allies and neighbors, except Germany."

Regarding the uncertain Polish elections, Bierut stated that the "elections in Poland will be held on the most democratic basis as soon as the repatriation task is completed, perhaps in a few months."

The press conference was based on a series of questions which the foreign correspondents had presented. An interpreter translated these questions to Bierut, who spoke Polish throughout the interview. The first question was answered last by Bierut.

"You have asked me to give a brief history of my life," said Bierut. "I find it rather difficult to talk about myself."

He then related that he was a co-operative worker in 1914 and later became chairman of a food co-operative in Lublin. He added that the co-operative developed well in Poland "because conditions made it so," and that in due time he became president of a union of food co-operatives.

Bierut said that in 1940 an organization known as the Polish National Council was founded by a number of partisan organizations with the idea to change Poland's policy toward Russia. He ignored the fact, however, that Poland did have a nonaggression pact with Russia in 1939, when Russia attacked Poland in the rear while Germany, with whom Poland also had a pact, attacked the Polish country from the west. Bierut's only explanation about the formation of the Polish National Council was:

"The group felt that not only the policy up to that time was wrong but also that a war between the Allies and Russia would be wrong."

Bierut further related that at one of the first meetings of the council on December 21, 1943, in Warsaw, he was elected president of this council, and that subsequently when the Polish provisional government was established he was retained as president of the new government.

Poles in Warsaw and throughout the Polish hinterland stated that Bierut was a Communist and was dictated to by Moscow. They added that he ruled Poland despotically by decrees rather than in accordance with laws adopted by the people.

"The decrees are prepared in Moscow and handed over to Bierut for public announcement and enforcement," a Polish journalist declared in Poznan. "His talk about the great democratization of Poland is sheer propaganda to confuse the people outside of Poland. His goal is to communize Poland along the pattern of Russia."

A pamphlet, entitled "Slowniczek Polityczny dla Zolnierzy" (Political Dictionary for Soldiers), identified Bierut as the son of a worker. It did not state where Bierut was born, but referred to him only as an "illustrious co-operative leader" persecuted by the old Pilsudski government. It further stated that Bierut "assumed the duties of the president of the republic from July 22, 1944, earning the love of the entire nation," and that he "united the entire strength of the nation and under his leadership an understanding was reached among all of the democratic leaders of the country and outside it in the establishment of the government of national unity." The description concluded with the statement that "Bierut was awarded the highest Polish honor—the Grunwald Cross, first class," but did not state by whom or for what reason. It failed to state that he was a Comintern agent —working for the Communist party—since 1923.

Bierut announced his "council of ministers" on June 28, 1945. Twelve of the 20 ministries were awarded to members of the Communist Polish Workers party and the Polish Socialist party, close collaborators in shaping Polish economic, industrial and social life along communistic patterns.

The provisional government was heralded as being based on four political parties, constituting a so-called united Democratic bloc. The "mouthpiece" of this political coalition was the dynamic Gomolka, who ranted violently at any rumors that a political party outside of the bloc was being formed. The four original political parties set up within the provisional government were the Communist Polish Workers party, headed by Gomolka; the Polish Socialist party, the Peasant party and the Democratic party. Gomolka did not want any other political parties in Poland for fear that he might lose control of the political situation in the country. The provisional government adopted the names of the parties in existence before the war to establish the bloc to mislead the world that political freedom exists in Poland. Some old leaders were persuaded to join these parties to make them appear authentic and mislead public opinion, but many of the old political leaders frowned upon this invitation because they did not want to play the role of stooges in an undemocratic form of government. Gomolka and his aides immediately characterized the Poles refusing to join his bloc as "fascists" and "reactionaries," simply because their interpretation of democracy was "a government of the people, by the people and for the people," instead of "a government of the minority, by the minority and for the minority," as exists in Russia.

The Polish political pot burst when Stanislaw Mikolajczyk, vice-premier and minister of agriculture, announced the active existence of his new Polish Peasant party at a meeting in Poznan. Mikolajczyk was former premier of the Polish government in exile in London and continues to be extremely popular in Poland.

Mikolajczyk, in his Poznan talk on October 7, 1945, before the Polish Peasant party, declared:

"One party does not represent the whole nation. The value of the alliance (with Russia) depends on the cooperation of the largest number of Polish people.

"We would really be very sorry if the question of the alliance were the monopoly of only one party and not the whole nation.

"We have decided to co-operate loyally and honestly with all the parties forming the government of national unity and we shall keep our obligations. We will not meddle in other parties, but we would like other parties not to interfere in our party life. That does not mean that we are displeased when a party co-operating with us points out that this or that is not in order in our midst.

"If there are really reactionaries among us, and I claim there are not, I should like this told to us, and let them be pointed out by name, just as we will speak up when we see many such persons who acted as members of the old Pilsudski crowd but today act under another guise."

Thousands of Poles joyously hailed Mikolajczyk's speech and his new party, which really was not something new because the provisional government had not only taken away the titles of the original Peasant party but even the old name. It was for that reason that Mikolajczyk's party had to call itself the Polish Peasant party (PSL). Mikolajczyk's party intends to return to the old name when conditions will permit it because "everyone inside the country and abroad knows that the Peasant party is an old political organization with a tradition of 50 years."

When thousands of Poles quickly enrolled in Mikolajczyk's Polish Peasant party, Gomolka became considerably irked and fearful that he might lose control of the political situation in Poland. In a bitter speech before the Warsaw chapter of the Polish Workers party, on October 21, 1945, Gomolka charged that "support given by reactionaries to Mr. Mikolajczyk means that they treat Mr. Mikolajczyk as a jumping-off board for gaining authority for themselves."

"It becomes clear to everybody that reactionaries would like to give Mr. Mikolajczyk the part of the Trojan horse to play and it is in this character only that they wish to see him in the government of national unity and in the bloc of the democratic parties," continued Gomolka heatedly. "They want to destroy the whole democratic structure under the pretext that religion is attacked, in order that the bishop's miter and the black cassock should decide about everything regarding the state and the nation.

"There are still mummified Polish scientists and pedagogues among us who cannot understand the new democracy, nor the historical events they witness. There are only a few scientists and pedagogues which cannot understand the new democracy, nor the historical events they witness. There are only a few scientists who gave all their knowledge for the construction of the foundations for democracy's building and for its consolidation. There are many, alas, who wish to use their knowledge as dynamite to blow up those foundations."

While Gomolka sprinkled his talk abundantly with the word "democracy," he did not use it in the sense that it is used in America. "Democracy" to Gomolka means "restricted politics"—restricted to the political bloc set up by the provisional government exclusively, in the same manner as only the Communist party is allowed to function in Russia. The "foundations," which Gomolka was fearful of being "blown up," were the Communist decrees transmitted by Moscow to Bierut for announcement in Warsaw. "Reactionaries," so far as Gomolka was concerned, were any Poles who disagreed with these Communist decrees and defined democracy as we know it in America—a rule of the majority.

Gomolka's verbal assault on Mikolajczyk and his Polish Peasant party was followed up by mass arrests of party members and confiscation of party seals and membership cards. Secret police began raiding district offices of the party throughout the Polish hinterland. More than 100,000 persons were rounded up in the drive and thrown into prisons or concentration camps. The pretext used by government officials in jailing the Polish Peasant party members was the statement that they were suspected of crime and subversive activities. The arrests were being made on such a large scale that our own Secretary of State Byrnes disclosed on January 31, 1946, that Poland was being swept by political murders and that the United States had warned Warsaw to honor its pledges to conduct free elections. Byrnes told Washington newspapermen that he had been advised there had been a number of murders in which prominent members of political parties have been the victims.

"It is regrettable that the Polish security police appear to have been implicated in a number of cases," Byrnes stated.

Byrnes's statement was relayed by Gerald K. Keith, an aide of Ambassador Lane, to Foreign Minister Wincenty Rzymowski. Officials of the Polish provisional government were of the opinion that their regime is to remain permanently and did not desire any official Allied observers for the elections on the grounds that Poland is a "sovereign country" and can take care of its own internal affairs.

Liquidation and confusion were the chief processes by which the provisional regime sought to remain in power. In addition to having the Russian garrisons and the dreaded NKVD to assist it, the regime founded the "Ormo," or a citizens' voluntary reserve militia, comprising armed men 18 to 45 years old. Some 100,000 of these men, chiefly members of the Communist Polish Workers' party and the Polish Socialist party, were recruited to patrol the streets on election day. Polish government officials maintained that the "Ormo" was founded to assure "peaceful and orderly balloting."

It is all so reminiscent of the pattern used by the Nazis and other totalitarian regimes in their early days.

* * *

An indication of what sort of "free and unfettered" elections would be held in Poland could be judged from the so-called referendum held in Poland on June 30, 1946, designed by Moscow to mislead the world into the erroneous belief that voting in Poland can be free and honest.

Immediately after the mock referendum, Stanislaw Mikolajczyk, head of the opposition Polish Peasant party, pointed out the irregularities in voting and in counting of the ballots. He exhibited to foreign correspondents some 1,000 partly burned and destroyed ballots he said were salvaged from sewers and refuse heaps. He charged that many partly destroyed ballots with negative votes were dumped into the sewers and that around Warsaw alone thousands of ballots were burned or partly destroyed. He added that before, during and after the referendum government security police arrested more than 5,000 followers of his Peasant party, and that censorship of his party newspapers was so severe that he had no opportunity to reveal the truth except through statements to foreign correspondents.

The questions voted upon at the referendum were: (1) Do you want a one-house parliament? (2) Do you approve of the actions of the provisional regime nationalizing basic industries and agrarian reform? (3) Do you approve establishment of Poland's western borders on the Neisse and Oder rivers?

The puppet government announced that the majority of Poles had voted "yes" on all three questions. Mikolajczyk charged that the NKVD police had confiscated all his party literature demanding a negative vote on the question of a one-house parliament.

Ironically, the mock referendum asked approval of a western boundary gained at Germany's expense, but made no reference to the eastern boundary where Russia had taken away a vast territory from Poland. Many Poles voiced their strenuous objections to such an unfair referendum by writing on their ballots such phrases as "We want back Lwow and Wilno." The puppet government ruled that such ballots were invalid.

Just how "free" the referendum was may be concluded from reports emanating from behind the iron curtain at that time. American and British diplomats and newspapermen were informed that any Pole seen talking to them on referendum day would be arrested by security police and the Soviet-sponsored government in Poland ruled that any blank ballots would be counted as affirmative votes. Furthermore, the government denied a Mikolajczyk request that representatives from each of the six polling parties act as clerks. Instead, clerks were selected from lists presented by the 17 provincial councils of which all but three are Communist controlled.

The referendum proved beyond any reasonable doubt that "free and unfettered" elections in Poland under Russian occupation and under supervision of the ruthless NKVD security police would be unthinkable.

V

LEO—MESSENGER FOR MOSCOW— VISITS POLAND

Fear and terror grip the people in the Polish hinterland, but Moscow's American messenger—Leo Krzycki, vice president of the CIO's Amalgamated Clothing Workers union—saw nothing except peace, joy and contentment through his rimless, gold-braced spectacles when I met him in Poland.

Polish workers earned 25 to 50 zlotys a day, an extremely small stipend when you consider that a full meat dinner cost from 400 to 700 zlotys. Yet short, stocky, garrulous Krzycki, who did not have to thrive on the Polish worker's diet of black bread and potatoes—three times a day— because he had plenty of American union money, bragged that the Polish working masses were now enjoying "the greatest prosperity in history."

For bamboozling the public in America and Poland regarding the "new Polish era," Moscow's American "messenger boy" was allowed to wander about—in the company of Soviet agents—for about five months behind the "iron curtain," including Poland, Russia, Yugoslavia and Czecho-Slovakia. Krzycki started his role as Moscow's "messenger boy" in 1941, when he became a champion of Soviet policy.

Upon his return to America from behind the "iron curtain," Krzycki minced few words in narrating the details of his 90-minute interview with Stalin. He boasted to the American press that the Soviet dictator spent more time talking with him than with America's Secretary of State James Byrnes.

Krzycki's biggest assignment as "messenger boy" for Moscow came about as follows:

On July 25, 1944, Russia announced its recognition of Boleslaw Bierut's Polish National Council formed at Moscow, empowering it also to administer civil affairs in Poland. Two days later the new Polish government's press bureau in Moscow began to send a steady stream of cablegrams thousands of miles away to Krzycki in Milwaukee.

Moscow was wiring to Krzycki the complete text of the Soviet-sponsored Polish regime's manifesto—22 pages —for two whole days, in addition to other cables recalling German atrocities.

Krzycki stated at the time when he was receiving Moscow's cables that the information came to him for circulation throughout the United States to keep Americans informed of activities of the new Polish provisional government.

The Russian government obviously selected Krzycki to lay the groundwork for the reception of the new Polish government among Polish-Americans, who a short time ago in Buffalo, N. Y., had organized the Polish American Congress to campaign for a free and independent Polish nation.

Disclosure of his part in the changing Polish picture was made by Krzycki on July 30, 1944, as head of the American Polish Labor Council. He explained at the

time that the council was formed in January of that year
to counteract bad feeling among Polish workers in America
toward each other, which, he claimed, was bred by "an
anti-Roosevelt administration attitude" by the Polish
government in exile in London and due to the London
group's attitude in the Polish-Russian border dispute.

The Moscow cables—now that the Soviet-sponsored
Polish provisional government was announced—told
Krzycki what to do in these words:

"The hour has arrived to visit retribution on Germany
for Poland's torments and sufferings, for burned villages
and demolished towns, for wrecked churches for exe-
cutions . . .

"Rise to the struggle for freedom . . .

"Rise, so that Poland will never again be threatened
with German invasion . . .

"Rise for a lasting peace, for creative labor, for prosperity . . ."

Krzycki did rise as his Moscow cables instructed him
to do. He left a few days after receiving the messages to
tour America and offer his Moscow material to the daily
press, to the labor union press with large Polish mem-
berships, to the Slavic press in America, and lectured
wherever he found willing audiences to listen. While
Krzycki thus traveled over the United States trying his
utmost to spread his Moscow propaganda, most Polish
Americans and most of the Polish press in America assailed
his Moscow affiliation in strong language.

Seven months before Krzycki received the new Polish
government's manifesto from Russia, his "home chapter"
(Milwaukee County) of the American Slav Council,
divorced itself from the national body on the grounds

that the latter was dominated by "communistic influences."

The "divorce" took place on Dec. 20, 1943, in an uproarious session. Sixteen council delegates of Krzycki's "home chapter"—including eight Polish delegates—wound up the stormy meeting by adopting three resolutions.

The first resolution condemned the un-American activities of certain individuals and organizations within the council in seeking "to divert the activity of affiliated organizations and exploit them to further the imperialistic aims of Soviet Russia." The resolution declared that the local council has now severed connections with the national and midwest committees of the American Slav Council.

The second resolution condemned the Milwaukee chapter of the Council of American-Soviet Friendship for prominently displaying, at the village fair of the Slav Council held in the Bohemian Hall in Milwaukee on Nov. 28, 1943, a map of Russia showing eastern Poland and the Baltic states as an integral part of the Soviet Union.

In the third resolution the local council decided that "certain groups"—that is, the Communist groups—whose activities do not fall within the aims of the organization, be excluded from the call for the next annual meeting of the council.

Frank E. Gregorski, then an assistant district attorney, who presided, announced at the meeting that the council would continue to carry on its strictly social activity as originally intended—that is, without discussion of international issues. He said there had been no trouble in the organization until certain communistic influences had insisted on bringing in issues involving the war. It was

charged by Polish delegates at the meeting that "Communists" connected with "certain unions" had "wormed their way" into the organization.

Who is Leo Krzycki, whose "home chapter" charged his American Slav Council with being dominated by "communistic influence" and whom Moscow delegated as the "recipient" of the new Polish provisional goverment's 22-page manifesto in July, 1944, long before the end of the war?

Krzycki, who some 37 years ago championed the cause of Socialism in soapbox talks, was born in Milwaukee of Polish parents. He is 67 years old. In 1904 he was made the international president of the Lithographer Press Feeders' union; from 1912 to 1916 he served as Socialist alderman in Milwaukee and from 1918 to 1920 as undersheriff. For more than 35 years he has been active in organization work for the Socialist party and labor unions. For 25 years he has been an organizer also for the Amalgamated Clothing Workers and a member of their executive board since 1922.

Well known for his ability to inspire inexperienced strikers, he has been "loaned" by the Amalgamated to many other labor groups. In 1933 he organized what he called "the shirt tail revolution," touring the Pennsylvania hills with a picked band of young workers to organize the shirt shops and other garment shops, among people who had never heard of a union.

In 1937 Krzycki spoke at a Chicago CIO mass meeting that preceded rioting in which five persons were killed and more than 100 injured near the strike-bound Republic Steel Corporation's South Chicago plant. A Chicago newspaper implied that his speech incited the 2,000 strikers and sympathizers to menace police guarding the plant. This Krzycki vigorously denied.

The Amalgamated's latest "loan" of Krzycki was to the Polish provisional government to influence the Polish workers to join the unions set up by Bierut and his colleagues of the Communist Polish Workers party and the Polish Socialist party. I met Krzycki in Warsaw, Poland, in October, 1945, and had lengthy conversations with him about his work in that war-stricken country.

One night I asked Krzycki, "Leo, why did you come to Poland?"

"To bring cheer and hope to the weary Polish workers," replied Krzycki. "At my age I could and should take it easy at home and spend my time with my grandchildren whom I love so dearly. But I felt deep in my heart that I must come here to Poland to assist the masses of Poles who have been victimized for centuries of the wealth they earned by large landowners and foreign capitalists.

"With the new Polish regime in existence, I am going out to all the Polish workers and peasants and tell them that henceforth they can keep the fruits of their labor. That's as it should be. The Poles have a great future ahead because the wealth will remain here instead of going to foreign interests."

I explained to Krzycki, who had developed into a "silver tongue" orator through years of soapbox speech making, that I had traveled extensively in Poland prior to his arrival in Warsaw and discovered great dissatisfaction among the Polish city dwellers and peasants with the policies and decrees of the Bierut government. I told him that the Poles everywhere were complaining to me about not receiving UNRRA relief goods and better-paying jobs unless they joined the Communist Polish

Workers party. I likewise informed him that the peasants had complained about the government taxes in the form of food and crop requisitions and that the Poles reported that Russian soldiers were stripping factories in the new Poland.

"Is that so?" was Krzycki's reply to all this.

One day Krzycki boasted in front of the news-stand in the Polonia Hotel:

"Isn't it wonderful that so many newspapers are being published here in Poland! And yet, you hear so much criticism about the Polish press from outside Poland."

When I told Krzycki that the newspapers were all censored and that even censorship of news copy of foreign correspondents existed in Poland, Krzycki replied, "Is that so? I didn't know that!"

The Polish government-controlled newspapers played up Krzycki's arrival and activities in Poland. The *Kurier Codzienny*, in its October 25, 1945, edition, stated:

"During his stay in Lodz, Leo Krzycki, the leader of Polish workers in America, gave an interview to the PAP (the aptly-named Polish government news agency) and said that 'reactionaries were trying to stir up action against Poland's present government in America. As a result, help which might have come here long ago is stopped.' On his return to America, he promised to present the real state of affairs in Poland."

The *Dziennik Ludowy* discussed Krzycki as follows, in its October 23 edition:

"Leo Krzycki made a speech in Lodz on the 21st at a meeting of the Polish food industries. He expressed his friendly feelings for the Soviets. America has to learn from the Polish workers unity both political and social. Until this is done the American masses will not be able to take advantage of all benefits."

One Sunday night Krzycki boasted that he had a four-hour interview with President Bierut.

"It was the longest interview that the president has had with any American," said Krzycki.

When I asked him what Bierut and he discussed at the conference, Krzycki replied: "I cannot tell you anything about what was discussed. A news release will be given out to the Polish papers by Polpress (government news agency replaced in name by PAP) regarding our conference."

Krzycki blushed when I reminded him that a few days ago he had boasted about the "great freedom of press in Poland" and that now he himself became "a victim of the censorship that I encountered daily while in Poland." He was ordered not to talk about his conference with Bierut for publication. The government agency instead was to prepare a statement on the conference for the press.

Several days later "news" of the conference Krzycki had with President Bierut "broke" in the Polish press. Warsaw newspapers, in response to the "directive" of the government, headlined the conference on their front pages.

While Krzycki was being quoted in the Polish press as telling Bierut that "lately many newspapers in America are beginning to write favorably about Poland," editorials in the newspapers of Poland were sharply castigating foreign correspondents for writing "unfavorably about conditions in Poland."

One day Krzycki, in his room at the Polonia Hotel in Warsaw, read part of his reports on Poland addressed to the late Sidney Hillman, his CIO boss, and asked me for my opinion. I advised Krzycki that his reports on "the great unity and great freedom in Poland" sounded fantastic and contrary to the conditions I had found throughout my travels in the Polish hinterland.

Krzycki became national chairman of the American Polish Labor Council—definitely a minority group of Polish Americans of leftist tendencies—when that group came into being in Cleveland, Ohio, in January, 1944. At that time Krzycki frankly admitted that now he had taken "hold of a real bundle of nettles." He explained that the Polish Labor Council was organized "to give voice to sentiments of American workingmen of Polish descent" on the relations between Soviet Russia and the Polish government in exile in London.

"Our government recognizes the Polish government in exile, so we are not picking a fight with the exiled government," Krzycki stated in January, 1944. "We propose to show that the exiled government does not represent the overwhelming sentiment of the people in Poland who till the soil and man the factories."

Thus did Krzycki and his pro-Soviet American Polish Labor Council lay the groundwork in January, 1944, in America for the "reception" of the Soviet-sponsored Polish provisional government, whose 22-page manifesto Krzycki received at his home in Milwaukee from Moscow six months later.

After leaving Poland in the fall of 1945, Krzycki proceeded to Russia, where he conferred with Stalin and Molotov about his work in behalf of the Polish provisional government.

Upon his return to Milwaukee from Europe, Krzycki was pictured on February 6, 1946, with Poland's Polonia

Restituta medal, awarded him by Bierut for pleading the cause of the new Polish government set up by Russia. He was also quoted as saying:

"Stalin wants American workers of Slav extraction. He wants to help them out if they are unemployed in the United States—wants to know if Slavs over here who are good mechanics will help Russia out for a couple of years by going there to work for Russia.

"Poland is not dominated by Russia. Her two big labor parties, the Polish Workers Party and the Polish Socialist Party, for the first time are co-operating like blood brothers, putting forth a united labor front. Led by them, the Polish laborer is producing more than before the war.

"Six political parties are in Poland now and they will have freedom to state their aims, for Poland will be given the right to choose her way. Russia, however, must have a transportation route through Poland to her zone in Germany, and Russian soldiers will remain in Poland for a while, but in the same manner that Americans and British are in Germany . . . Russia will give Poland her own regime as soon as possible."

Krzycki said nothing about the lack of freedom of press and the system of "chartering" political parties in Poland. Nor did he say anything about the wholesale political arrests of members belonging to Mikolajczyk's Polish Peasant party or about the secret police raids upon the offices of that party. Neither did he mention the fact that Bierut awarded 12 of the 20 ministries of the Soviet sponsored Polish provisional government to members of the Communist Polish Workers party (which before the war had only 5 out of 444 seats in the Polish Diet) and the Polish Socialist party, its close collaborator.

He failed likewise to state the abuses on the part of Bierut's government involving the distribution of UNRRA goods.

Krzycki similarly failed to discuss the fear in which the Poles were living then as a result of the activities of Poland's secret police operating under the dreaded Soviet NKVD. While he was being quoted as saying that "six political parties are in Poland now and they will have freedom to state their aims," Larry Allen of the Associated Press, with whom I had many discussions while in Poland in the fall of 1945, reported the same day (February 5, 1946) in a delayed dispatch from Warsaw that a new drive was started by "Poland's secret police, whose net already may have swept from 75,000 to 100,000 persons into jails and prisons."

While Krzycki boastfully represented himself as a leader of Polish Americans, virtually the whole Polish language press in America severely assailed him for his pro-Soviet tendencies.

A Milwaukee Polish language newspaper (February 6, 1946) bitterly criticized Krzycki for making a bid in behalf of Stalin to Slav workers to come to Russia and work there for a couple of years. In a sharply worded editorial to its American readers of Polish descent, the newspaper stated:

"Krzycki, as it appears, wants to help Russia. He returned from Moscow, where he undoubtedly received instructions. It appears that Krzycki will follow the Milwaukee Nazi (Eugene J. Buerk, who was deported to Germany in 1941 for recruiting Americans of German descent to work in German factories). Many workers went (to Germany) and bitterly regretted it since. Krzycki wants Poland to be tied up with Russia as a Soviet puppet.

Don't let any of you (Americans) betray the USA in behalf of Stalin.

"He (Krzycki) returned to this country, where the worker is free, where our banner is honored everywhere as a symbol of peace, brotherly might, where there is freedom for the poor and rich alike, to plant Communism."

Krzycki participated in a radio debate and gave a number of talks in which he maintained that the "Poles are enjoying freedom for the first time in history," but he found only an insignificant number of auditors gullible enough to swallow his party line as gospel truth.

Although Krzycki posed as a "champion" of a "democratic" Poland, he never took part in the activities of the American Relief for Poland organization, which gathered millions of dollars in relief goods for the Polish war sufferers. Neither did he take part in the Polish American Congress, organized in Buffalo, N. Y., in 1944 to campaign for a truly free and sovereign Poland.

Instead, Krzycki was strongly pro-Russian, voicing approval of Stalin's absorption of the war-weary Polish nation and spouting insidious falsehoods about the so-called "new Poland," which he visited when I was there in the fall of 1945.

* * *

At a rally of the Third American Slav Congress held in New York on September 22, 1946, Krzycki boasted to the delegates that he brought a "personal message of greeting" from Marshal Tito of Yugoslavia, who a few weeks before made little of the shooting down of five American fliers over his country. The pro-Soviet delegates to the Slav congress booed at the mention of the name of Secretary of State Byrnes and applauded their hero, Henry Wallace, who a few days before was ousted by

President Truman from the cabinet post of secretary of commerce for his speech criticizing the American foreign policy and urging appeasement of Russia. Attending the conclave were representatives of the Soviet government and its satellites, Poland, Czecho-Slovakia, Bulgaria and Yugoslavia.

While Krzycki espoused Stalin's establishment of the Communist puppet governments in the small European countries, Americans of Polish descent vigorously assailed Krzycki for assuming the role of "mouthpiece" in their behalf.

The Polish American Labor Council, headed by J. K. Wieczorek of Chicago, in an open letter to Krzycki challenged his representation of "600,000 Polish American workers" and inquired in a long series of questions: "Did you and your 'organized American Polish workers' at any time 'co-operate' with the German Bund, Russian Communists and Italian Fascists, calling strikes all over this country, when the late President Roosevelt started to prepare America against Hitler-Stalin-Mussolini?"

Unlike Krzycki's approval of the Soviet-sponsored policies in Poland, the Polish American Labor Council, headed by Wieczorek, differed sharply with those policies in "A Polish Appeal" addressed to President Truman on December 1, 1945. The "Appeal," in part, stated:

"At the present, with the quiet consent of the world's leading democracies, under the vigilant eye of the NKVD, Soviet Secret Police and the Red Army are doing everything so that Little Poland is undergoing a speedy process of virtual sovietization, to prepare well 'the democratic unfettered elections' in which Democratic and anti-Nazi parties shall have the right to vote. According to the Yalta promises . . . it is putting a premium on murder, terror and oppression. Under these circumstances it will not be an election by ballots, but by BULLETS, hostages and concentration camps. This process, the Russian process of democratic changes, is at present going on in Poland . . .

"Mr. President, please use your great influence and power to see that our first ally POLAND gets a chance at democracy, as well as all our allies, and that this will come as soon as possible, not after many, many years to come . . ."

The ominous message dated December 1, 1945, to President Truman of an election "not by ballots, but by BULLETS," became a reality on Sunday, January 19, 1947. Krzycki, who offered me great opportunity and a great future if I would join his ranks, will never be able to live down the role he played as Stalin's messenger in propagandizing the "new democracy" of the puppet totalitarian Polish government.

A Warsaw Shrine

VI

THE STATUS OF THE CHURCH IN POLAND

How did Poland, which is predominantly Catholic, become Christianized? What is the status of the Church today?

Poland's eventful history begins in the year 842 when the Slav tribe of Polanie, dwelling since time immemorial on the central European plain cut by the rivers Elbe, Oder, Warta and Vistula, elected Piast, the wheelwright, for their ruler. Piast's grandson, King Mieszko I, received baptism and introduced Christianity and western civilization in Poland in 966. With this event Poland became the leader among the Slavic tribes occupying the areas east of the Elbe.

Historians emphasize that Mieszko's act of adopting Christianity wrought consequences that were of more than purely Polish interest. Chronicling the conversion of Poland to Christianity, one historian wrote:

"As far back as Charlemagne there had begun an expansion of the Teutonic nations toward the east. This is that vast movement called the 'Drang nach Osten,' or 'the pressure toward the east.' The Slavs between the Elbe and the Oder, less warlike, smaller in stature than the Teutons, not well organized, relatively ill armed, were slowly subjugated.

65

"When Otto I of Saxony was crowned emperor in 962 his already great power was so enhanced that he became a menace to all the Slavs east of him.

"Mieszko (King of Poland) soon saw that the only means of preventing the enslavement or extermination of his people lay in the same alliance that had so strengthened Otto, that with the church. For, as long as the Poles were heathens, they were the legitimate prey of any Christian king, but as Christians they would at once be on a par with other western nations. Their entering the fold of the Catholic church would deprive Otto of a valid excuse for incursions into their territory, win the sympathy of the other nations of Christendom, and gain the favor and advocacy of the pope. By calling in monks from France and Italy they would forge valuable ties with those lands.

"These were the motives prompting Polish adhesion to the Christian church. The results were not only good but momentous. The nation became really and increasingly Christian. In the first centuries of Christianity the people received the light of Latin learning and the advantages of Western civilization, largely from the hands of Benedictine, Eremite, and Cistercian monks from the monasteries of Liege, Cluny and Monte Cassino. The pope became their advocate.

"But two results even more far reaching than these were determined by this step. First, in deciding to become Catholic, Poland chose to face West. The Czechs had already taken the same step. But when Poland also became Roman Catholic, a second, less desirable effect was permanently to divide Slavdom, for most of the other Slav nations, the Russians, the Bulgarians, and the Serbs, are of the Eastern Orthodox faith. However, notwithstanding certain important consequences resulting from the division of the Slavs in the matter of religion, it was good for all the world that in accepting the Christian faith Poland came in through the western and Latin door and not through the more backward and orientalized Orthodox one, with its absolutism, Greek alphabet and decaying Byzantinism."

In 1683, the Polish king, Jan Sobieski, ran the risk of Russian aggression to go to the assistance of Vienna, besieged by the Turks. By his victory, one of the world's decisive battles, Poland preserved Europe for Christianity. A "Te Deum" was sung in the Cathedral of St. Stephen in Vienna, and these words were uttered from the cathedral: "There was a man sent from God whose name was John." Later, Poland signed a pact of perpetual friendship with Turkey, the only state that never recognized the partitions of Poland, keeping an empty seat at all diplomatic receptions for the "temporarily absent" Polish ambassador.

Throughout Poland's stormy history, including the historic partitions of 1772, 1793, and 1795, the Poles remained fervent Catholics. Historians point out that this unity of religion running through the years made "for the survival of Poles as Poles—and indeed for the survival of Europe as Europe."

The Germans were motivated by this fact in introducing the worst religious persecution campaign in Poland's history during the occupation years from 1939 to 1945 in their attempt to destroy the Polish people once and for all as a nation.

The Germans suppressed seven Polish dioceses and deported or imprisoned seven bishops and threw 90% of the clergy into concentration camps. The Gestapo also executed a large number of priests. In Oswiecim alone 1,500 priests died of maltreatment. The Germans closed churches and deprived many millions of Catholics entirely of religious services, in a country where more than 70% of the people are Catholic.

Now that the Germans were defeated and gone from Poland, what is the status of the Catholic church in Poland?

First of all, the pre-war relations between the Catholic church and the Polish government no longer exist. Secondly, the provisional government shortly after its regime began abrogated Poland's concordat with the Vatican.

High Catholic clergymen in Poland stated that in their opinion the actions of Bierut's provisional government smack of Communism.

"The Polish people are gradually losing their freedoms and are being led into Communism," said one of the clergymen. "We do not have a government of the people, by the people and for the people as you have in America."

The Communists are out to destroy Christianity in Poland," said another clergyman. "They feel that by destroying Christianity in Poland their first bulwark against Communism will be overcome."

In their Sunday sermons at masses the Catholic priests throughout Poland are exhorting their parishioners, "Don't ever give up your religion no matter what the future may hold in store for you."

The tenseness that prevailed between the Polish provisional government and the Catholic church was evident everywhere in Poland. High clergymen stated that they were yearning for reading matter from America to find out what the people of other Christian countries were doing to help alleviate the wretchedness of the Poles. They inquired whether any religious aid was being organized in America to help save Christianity in Poland.

In the fall of 1945 when the government declared only civil marriages legal in Poland, the Catholic *"Tygodnik Powszechny"* (The Universal Weekly)) vigorously attacked the government for its policy. In the same issue a scathing article entitled "Filozofia Marksizmu" (The Philosophy of Marxism) appeared, attacking some of the principles that are being put into being in Poland.

"The present government is watching the church closely," said one Catholic church leader, "But there has been no open conflict. It would be dangerous for the government to cause such a church conflict because the internal situation in Poland would get out of control, since Poland is predominantly Catholic.

"Cardinal Hlond has not officially notified the government of his return to Poland because as the head of the Catholic church in Poland he was already established in his seat before the existence of the new government."

There is an acute shortage of Catholic priests in Poland, but Russian interference is curtailing the training of new priests in at least one seminary. A high clergyman stated:

"Now that efforts are being made to educate more priests to replace those executed by the Germans, the church is hindered because the Russians have occupied one of our largest seminaries and the Red Army has no intention of leaving the seminary."

Communists were delighted with the destruction of the large beautiful churches of Warsaw, but the Poles continued attending services daily in the wrecked church basements or in the rectories. The Poles in their wretchedness appeared to be mindful that their unity and survival, as proven by their history, depends on their religion. The Communists are mindful of that fact, too, and therefore are doing all they can to interfere with religion without creating an open conflict with the church.

* * *

There is little doubt that the Church in Poland has an ominous future as a result of the fake elections won on January 19, 1947, by the Communist-dominated political bloc. An indication of what is in store for the Church was evidenced even weeks before the bogus election results were disclosed when two priests late in 1946 were sentenced to death by the Polish provisional government on charges that they participated in "underground activities." The puppet government for "convenience" uses the word "underground" in connection with any Pole voicing resentment against the decrees and ruthless dealings of the government.

VII

TWELVE MILLION DEAD IN SIX YEARS

World War II shrank Poland's population from 35,000,000 to 23,000,000, an extremely heavy price for the freedom which the Poles hoped to procure at the close of the war, but did not get. Figures are not available to show to what extent Germany and Russia are each responsible for the loss of 12,000,000 Poles between 1939 and 1946. If figures were available, however, the ledger would show that Germany and Russia are both responsible for the deaths of millions of Poles.

The man who will go down in Polish history as the cruelest ruler of Poland will be fat, brutal Hans Frank, German governor-general of Poland for more than five years—1939 to 1945. Throughout his reign of terror Frank was known as the "Butcher of Warsaw" because he directed the establishment of the unheard of mass extermination plants in Poland. He was largely responsible for the shrinking of Warsaw's population from 1,500,000 to 400,000.

"Butcher Frank" slaughtered more than 3,000,000 Jews in Poland during the war. In the fall of 1945, only 80,000 Jews were still living in the Polish country out of some 4,000,000 alive before the German war machine started to roll on September 1, 1939.

Frank lived royally in the famous ancient palace of the Wawel while issuing "slaughtering orders" for millions of Poles. The limestone hill of Wawel, picturesquely situated on the Vistula River and dominating the whole town, stands at the southern end of the city of Krakow.

The Wawel is accessible from Grodzka Street and the Planty parkway. The place is dear to every Pole, for it was the residence of the Polish rulers in the times of Poland's greatest power, up to the seventeenth century, and afterwards became the national Pantheon.

"Butcher Frank" headed a "special list" of six most important German criminals whom the Poles wanted to hang at the first opportunity. The other five were Kruger, governor-general of Krakow; Zorner, district governor of Lublin; Dr. Ludwig Fischer, district governor of Warsaw; Ernst Kundt, district governor of Radom, and Dr. Wachter, governor of Lwow.

Frank was born on May 23, 1900, in Karlsruhe, Germany, being 39 years old when Hitler appointed him governor-general of Poland on Oct. 12, 1939.

He and his fellow "supermen" fled their luxurious living quarters in haste at the rapid approach of the Russians early in 1945, and did not demolish any of the historic buildings that make up the Wawel. However, Frank and his henchmen did considerable looting of treasured art objects, according to Tadeusz Mankowski, director of the state museum at Wawel.

Mankowski said that he already had put the buildings in sufficient order, after Frank's departure, to open them as a museum to visitors. Mankowski said that efforts would be made to bring back from Germany all of the art objects belonging to the Wawel that could be found.

Hundreds of nuns and other Poles from various parts of Poland were touring the Wawel on one of the days I visited it.

Near the entrance to the Wawel one still sees the monument of Thaddeus Kosciuszko, Polish hero of the American Revolutionary War and leader of the Polish struggle for independence in the years of 1792-94. The royal castle dates back to the tenth century, but was then partly built of wood. The cathedral was begun a century later. Guns taken from the Bolsheviks during the war in 1920, still stand in the courtyard of the castle.

Mankowski said that Frank occupied the Wawel palace or castle that had been used in pre-war Poland by the president of the Polish republic whenever he visited Krakow. Frank had a white, modernistic bathtub brought from Germany and installed in a washroom adjoining the bedroom. His bed had a red, plush bedspread and a red plush canopy over it.

"Throughout his five years of occupancy of the royal palace," said Mankowski, "Frank had the Poles constantly washing the walls and polishing the marble."

The palace was "spick and span" when I saw it.

Frank's daughter, according to Mankowski, slept in the bed of Zygmunt I, one of the earliest kings of Poland. His son occupied a room in one of the castle nooks. Dissatisfied with the art work on the ceiling, the son ordered it to be covered with white paint. Since then the Poles have removed the white paint and the original art work again may be viewed by the visitors.

"Butcher Frank" relaxed from his "slaughtering" by frequently attending movies in the beautiful senate hall of the castle, formerly used by the Poles for receptions and balls in pre-war Poland. Ancient banners seized from the Knights of Teutonic Order in the Battle of Grunwald in 1410 still hang in the hall. Likewise, are hanging priceless Dutch tapestries and the huge Turkish tents which the Poles captured centuries ago in victorious battles.

Polish artists were sketching in the castle courtyard, an activity Frank had strictly prohibited during his reign of terror in Poland. The beautiful castle yard of the Wawel, with its arched entrances, has regained its original aspect, when in it were held tournaments of the medieval knights. A school of architecture for Krakow University students is conducted at the Wawel now due to a shortage of classrooms at the university.

Mankowski said that Frank and his cohorts stole prized works of art from the cathedral on the Wawel, considered the richest church in all of Poland, considering the quantity of artistic and historical objects of every period which it contains. The cathedral, housing the graves of Polish kings and national heroes, was built in the Roman style in the eleventh century and reconstructed in the fourteenth in the Gothic style. It has quite lost its original character in the numerous restorations that followed. Eighteen chapels were built around it, either in the Renaissance or the Baroque style. These were the greatest ornaments of the cathedral. Some of these Frank removed, but left undisturbed were the splendid tombs of kings, bishops and nobles, beneath the cathedral, sculptured by Polish, Italian, German, Danish and French artists.

The crypt in the palace cathedral contains the graves of the late Marshal Joseph Pilsudski, Gen. Kosciuszko, the famed poets, Adam Mickiewicz and Julius Slowacki, and scores of national heroes, kings of Poland and other great men. Gothic and Renaissance decorations surround the graves.

In addition to watching the movies in the senate hall of the Wawel palace, Frank would also relax from his monotonous job of issuing death orders by attending a casino which he established in an old building at Rynek gl. 16 in downtown Krakow. This building formerly was a dining rendezvous for Polish nobility dating as far back as four hundred years ago. The original proprietor had a reputation of giving a golden goblet to each nobleman who visited the place.

Frank restored this building into a two-story clubroom for 25 of his specially picked cronies. He furnished the premises with a half dozen ancient tile stoves, about eight feet high, which were brought from Polish palaces. The exclusive "Frank's Casino" is now operated as a restaurant by Kazimierz Ksiazek, who on my visit there led me through all the rooms of the casino, explaining every detail.

"Whenever Hans Frank came to the casino," said Ksiazek, "German 'supermen' were atop the building with machine guns ready for action in the event of a sudden Polish attack on him.

"Frank would never alight from his car in front of the entrance. Instead, his chauffeur would speed quickly into the gateway alongside the casino and into the inner courtyard. German soldiers knew in advance when Frank was coming so that the gateway would be opened for him at the right moment of his entry."

Ksiazek said that there was no doubt that Frank was a "scared rabbit" in Krakow despite the thousands of "supermen" he had around him.

"I don't think Frank was a happy man even though he lived like a king in a palace and had the best casino in all of Poland," said Ksiazek. "How could he be happy when his conscience gave him no peace and hundreds of Poles walked around Krakow with revolvers under their coats waiting for the right moment to kill him."

A favorite story of the Poles in Krakow centers around "Butcher Frank" and Cardinal (then an archbishop) Adam S. Sapieha, who is regarded as a hero in Poland because of his courageous stand against the German oppression. One day Frank had invited the Cardinal to the Wawel palace and dined him at a sumptuous dinner. In return for his "hospitality," the prelate invited Frank to his chancery for a dinner. Frank did not remain to partake of it, but left in a huff. The "dinner" consisted chiefly of potatoes, black bread and similar unappetizing food, the only kind the Polish people were allowed under the German occupation. Cardinal Sapieha told Frank, "I regret that I cannot serve you as well as you served me at your palace dinner, for we Poles are an occupied country and to the invaders go the best food while we must thrive chiefly on potatoes and black bread."

Cardinal Sapieha is 80 years old. He "got into Frank's hair" often because of his patriotism. He defied the Germans time and again to kill him when they became incensed at him, but they did not dare execute him. As a result, he is more popular than ever. Pope Pius XII elevated him to the rank of cardinal after the war.

Americans, who are firm believers in freedom of religion, will fully appreciate Cardinal Sapieha's bitterness toward the "Butcher of Warsaw" and his henchmen, after reading about Frank's religious and cultural persecution in Poland.

Frank suppressed seven Polish dioceses in Poznan, Gniezno, Wroclawek, Plock, Pelplin, Lodz and Katowice. He deported the seven bishops or imprisoned them. He

put 90% of the clergy into concentration camps. With
the aid of the Gestapo, he executed more than 2,000
priests. In the horrible Oswiecim concentration camp
alone 1,500 priests died of maltreatment. Churches were
closed and many millions of Catholics were entirely
deprived of religious services in a country where some
75% of the people are Catholics.

Fat, brutal Frank closed the Polish universities,
professional and technical educational institutions, high
schools and all private schools, thereby denying completely
or delaying education to millions of Polish youths for
nearly six years. Under Frank's orders, German specialists
came into Poland and looted libraries, museums, scientific
centers and laboratories. The loot was then transported
to Germany. Ruling that the "Poles do not require
learning," Frank issued this statement:

"The Poles do not need universities or secondary
schools. The Polish territories are to be transformed into
an intellectual desert."

Cardinal Sapieha spoke about Frank's ruthlessness.
He stated that in 1942 Frank had ordered the burning
of 348 villages to the ground and ploughing them under
like Lidice; 1,080 villages evacuated and all the inhabitants
either killed or deported.

Frank routed Jews from their long established homes
into the ghettos and walled them in. The Jews then were
burned alive or shot. Other Jews were transported to
concentration camps for ultimate death there.

Under Frank's regime, the confiscation of public and
private property in Poland was complete. The Germans
not only took all the land, stores and workshops away
from the Poles, but they also confiscated their household
furniture and personal effects, suck as furs, jewelry,

clothing and other personal items. Small farmers were evicted. German colonists replaced the Poles driven from their farms and businesses. The Poles were used as slave labor and exploited by the Germans, receiving little pay, and even this was taxed a flat 15% in addition to other heavy taxes, social insurance, dues and "contributions." Their pay on the average was half of what Germans received for the same work, but their hours were longer and they were allowed no holidays.

Frank allowed no fuel to be sold to the Poles. Their food rations were less than half of what the Germans in Poland received. And when slowdowns in production occurred—an important feature of underground resistance —Frank ordered that the Poles' food ration cards be withdrawn. Polish workers, whose output fell below 60% of the German production standard, received no ration cards and had to starve with their families. Workers whose output was 68%, received one-third of the concentration camp ration, and those whose production was 80%, received 50% of the German ration.

An eyewitness account of how the Poles lived in horror and fear in Krakow under Frank's "regime of terror" was vividly described by Mrs. Stefania Germak, sister of Thaddeus Borun, 329 E. Rosedale Av., Milwaukee, Wis., an acquaintance of mine.

Mrs. Germak, her husband, Joseph, and their son, George, 22, live in a small third-floor apartment at 10 Zielona Street. They formerly lived in another apartment but the Gestapo in 1942 drove them out to make living quarters for German civilians who came to live in Krakow. The Germaks were assigned to their present apartment, which was previously inhabited by Jews rounded up on Frank's orders and sent to the ghetto and subsequently liquidated. The Germans either killed or sent away to concentration camps some 42,000 Krakow Jews, according to Mrs. Germak.

"Neither at home nor in the street was one sure he would not find himself in prison the next day," said Mrs. Germak. "The Germans arrested men especially and threw them into prison or drove them away never to be heard from again and for no reason at all.

"The curfew in Krakow used to vary. Sometimes it would be 4 p.m., sometimes at 6 p.m., but nearly always it was 7 p.m., after which hour a Pole could not be found in the street without risking death.

"In our house the German police were looking for a Warsaw woman, who was to live with us. That was Jan. 12, 1945. They looked through the apartment and left. But from another apartment in the house they took the tailor, his wife and son, because they wrote to another son in America.

"The son who was at home belonged to the 'armia krajowa' (underground home army). The Germans shot this son in Oswiecim, the father died in prison, and the mother went mad in prison."

Mrs. Germak said that the Germans in August, 1944, fearing they were going to lose the war "evacuated all the offices and their office furniture from Krakow. They took the young Polish people with them."

"Jurek (George, her son) ran away from home at that time to hide in the woods with his school friends for four months," said Mrs. Germak tearfully. "As this cost too much, he had to come back and register for digging trenches.

"Through the worst months he and other young Poles dug in the snow and cold and in the mud those ditches near Plaszow. He had to walk four kilometers. He caught cold and was ill.

"Then father found him some work with a saddler who was working for the army, so they took him there and he did not have to work in the trenches. But this was already January, 1945, and soon, on the twenty-third, the Germans ran away from Krakow.

"The city did not suffer much damage. Only during the blowing up of the bridges on the Vistula the windows were broken and several shells destroyed some houses on Zwierzyniecka and in Debniki."

Mrs. Germak wept bitterly as she said, "No one in America can ever imagine how much we suffered under the brutal German occupation."

"Many of our neighbors and friends were shot on the street," she said, "for listening to radio broadcasts. One Sunday afternoon the Gestapo found 14 Poles playing cards to pass their time away. The Gestapo accused these Poles of 'holding a conspiracy meeting against the Reich,' forced them out into the street and shot every one."

One day while walking on a busy Krakow street in the latter part of October, 1945, I was stopped by a haggard old man who pushed up the sleeve of his coat and pointed to a tattooed number on his arm. "Oswiecim," he whispered, with a horrifying stare. I reached into my pocket and handed him 100 zlotys.

Oswiecim was "Butcher Frank's" largest "human extermination plant" in Poland.

I was taken on a tour of the concentration camp by Mieczyslaw Swider, a retired Polish Army major, who is commandant in charge of the preservation of it. It was a terrifying sight.

Measuring 42 square kilometers (about 26 square miles), the Oswiecim camp is surrounded by barbed wire fences, about 7 to 8 feet in height. The barbed wires, while the camp was in operation, were electrified. The camp is about one and a half kilometers from the district town of Oswiecim, which in the fifteenth century served as the capital of a principality of the Silesian Piasts.

Swider said that the camp would be preserved as a "monument to Hitler brutality," upon completion of a study being made by a commission in Krakow of the execution at Oswiecim of an estimated 6,500,000 Poles (including some 3,000,000 Polish Jews), Czechs, Frenchmen, Rumanians, Russians and Italians.

I found the Oswiecim camp for the most part in ruins, for the Germans in their hasty retreat from the advancing Russians dynamited the four crematories and adjoining "shower rooms" to destroy as much of the evidence of mass murder as possible.

Swider explained that the Germans would jam the victims into the "shower rooms" and turn on the gas to kill them. The bodies would then be carried to the crematories by conveyors and burned there, he said. Each crematory could burn 24 bodies at a time.

"There were so many gas victims, however, that the Germans could not keep up burning them in the crematories, so they began to burn the bodies in open pits," said Swider. "Children under five were not even gassed. Instead, the Germans threw them alive into the pit fires, frequently snatching them from the arms of their screaming mothers. This unheard of extermination of innocent children in the history of mankind illustrates the diabolical methods used by the Germans in their mad attempts to destroy the Polish nation.

"Before being sent into what appeared like 'shower rooms,' the victims were told to strip. They then were given towels and soap, presumably for bath purposes.

"The German soldiers would not shut the doors of the 'shower rooms' and turn on the gas until 2,000 victims were jammed into each 'shower room.' If the victims did not move into the rooms fast enough, the Germans would sick onto them wild dogs kept in the huge kennels there. Jews were used to haul out the dead bodies from the 'shower rooms' and place them on the conveyors leading to the crematories."

Ashes and small chips of human bone were scattered on the floors of the dynamited crematories. On the ground surrounding the crematories were parts of dentures, charred frames of glasses, coins, keys and other metal personal possessions, which Swider stated belonged to the victims.

Swider has Polish guards, armed with rifles, assigned to preserve the concentration camp because scores of vandals come there each day in search of gold teeth and other valuable objects amid the human ashes and rubble.

The rows of wooden barracks in which the "shower rooms" victims were temporarily held pending their death are still standing. Some of these have been occupied by the Russians after expelling the Germans from the territory. Russian soldiers have painted numerous colorful pictures on the barracks to transform them from "death cells" of a depressing atmosphere to gay living quarters. I was prohibited from visiting 20 brick two- and three-story buildings on the concentration camp site "because these buildings house German prisoners of war" under guard of Russian troops. Swider said that visitors are strictly prohibited by the Russian garrison from entering that area.

Swider said that the Germans had brought their victims in railroad freight cars leading directly into the camp. Sometimes entire Polish villages were emptied and the whole population brought to the camp. The train entered the camp under a red brick tower, soon called the "Tower of Death."

"Those who were husky and physically fit were sent to a nearby ammunition plant to work there until they became unfit and then were sent to the 'shower rooms,' " said Swider. "Many of the victims were also forced to work in a synthetic benzene plant, not far from Oswiecim, before being executed. The hair on the heads of the women were cut off before these women were executed. The hair was sent to Germany to aid in the 'war effort.' Some 4,000 Polish women, with their heads shaved, and their bodies like skeletons, but still alive, were found by Russians on their arrival at the camp. A mound of women's hair was also found at the camp.

"The Germans compelled the Jews to burn the victims in the crematories for a week. After a week's work the Jew himself was burned by the diabolical 'supermen.' "

Still standing were the kennels, where the Germans had kept their dogs and trained them to attack the "shower room" victims.

One of the camp guards working under Swider was Stanley, a 50-year-old Pole, who said that he escaped from Oswiecim after being confined there for 19 months. Stanley, displaying his tattooed number on his wrist, said that he and 90 other Poles ran away from a work farm which produced vegetables for the German officers. This farm was a few kilometers from the camp. Each day these

91 Poles were marched from the camp to the work farm and back.

"I saw the Germans throw many children under five years of age into the open pit fires while the children were alive because the Germans did not want to 'waste' any gas on these youngsters," Stanley told me.

Near-by Trzebinka was part of the Oswiecim concentration camp. At first the Germans used it for Belgians, then they executed English prisoners there. From 1942, Jews were put to death there. The crematorium at Trzebinka, like those at Oswiecim proper, are to be preserved.

"Butcher Frank" established an "extermination camp," similar to that at Oswiecim, in Majdanek, where he also gassed millions of Poles and burned their bodies in crematoriums. The Majdanek camp is to be preserved as a "monument to Hitlerism" also.

While the camps at Oswiecim and Majdanek were truly horrifying, "Butcher Frank's" most repulsive enterprise in Poland was his human soap factory at Wrzeszcz, near Gdansk (Danzig). Here Frank's laboratory technicians produced soap from human bodies, and women's purses and belts from human skins, sent as souvenirs to sweethearts and wives back home by the German soldiers.

If you were to visit this former "Institute of Hygiene" at Wrzeszcz, among other things you will see:

A vat filled with tanned human skin.

The soap factory with cut-up human bodies.

A body of a Polish sailor with tattooing on his chest representing a ship and this inscription, "God *is with us*, Polish Navy. Wicher. 1930."

A tank in which human bodies were boiled.

A vat in which the bodies were soaked. On the shelves skulls and bones.

A vat with bodies soaked in a caustic.

An incinerator in which the remains were burned.

Chunks of soap made from human bodies and the molds in which the "soap" was shaped and set.

This chapter recites only briefly how the "Butcher of Warsaw" liquidated Poland. History will require considerable time in telling the entire story of Frank's process of "slaughtering," for the Poles who are alive today are still uncovering new graves. For example, in October, 1945, the Poles found new graves in Grudiacz, where in 1939 some 600 Poles were murdered there by Frank's henchmen. Similar "graves" are being unearthed throughout Poland periodically.

SEARCHING FOR BODIES—FAMILIAR POLISH SCENE

VIII

WHY POLAND REMAINS A "KEG OF DYNAMITE"

With the departure of the "Butcher of Warsaw" and his Nazi henchmen, Poland still remains a "keg of dynamite."

Making detailed notes each day, I traveled deep into the Polish hinterland on a British truck and observed how the German menace was replaced by the Russian menace in Poland. Traveling with me were two British soldiers and two correspondents, Emlyn Williams, veteran war correspondent of *The Christian Science Monitor*, and Charles Lambert, staff reporter of *The London Daily Herald*. The trip was rough and uncertain because of gunfire at night. But it afforded me an opportunity to speak in Polish to housewives, laborers, farmers and local government officials and thus learn at first hand the true living conditions in postwar Poland.

The British soldiers were sent with the lorry by the British ambassador to Szczecin, the former German port of Stettin, which was the end of "Operation Eagle," a name given to the task of repatriating Poles from the British zone of occupation in Germany.

All roads leading from Hamburg to Szczecin were marked EU (Eagle Up), and ED (Eagle Down) for the return journey. The first convoy of British repatriated

87

Poles from Germany was scheduled to arrive in Szczecin on Oct. 14, and the two British soldiers attached to the British embassy left Warsaw to greet the British Army unit convoying the Poles into Szczecin.

After leaving Warsaw, the British lorry made its first stop at Grodzisk. The October sun had been quickly setting on this typically Polish provincial town as the lorry crew stopped to allow us to obtain a cup of coffee and some delicious Polish "ciastka" (pastries). We had a late start in leaving Warsaw on Friday afternoon, Oct. 12, and, consequently, we were ready for a light lunch.

Grodzisk is about 30 kilometers (less than 20 miles) from Warsaw, but our trip through Warsaw and the suburb Praga had taken us a bit longer than we had expected because of the extremely heavy traffic of migrants in and out of the Polish capital. The traffic was bottled up on the wooden bridge over the Vistula River.

As we were munching our "ciastka" and sipping our coffee (very much unlike American brewed coffee), a woman, who had heard me speak Polish to the cafe proprietor, rushed to our table and cried out in Polish, "Oh, sir, you are an American, are you not?" I replied, "Yes."

"I surely thought you were an American because of the fine clothes you are wearing," said the woman, about 40. "Nobody in all of Poland wears such fine clothes as you do."

I explained to her that the clothes I was wearing were ordinary clothes in America and their price modest.

"Nobody could buy such clothes here in Poland, for we have not seen such material in years," said the woman.

"Furthermore, we do not even have the money to buy the food which is priced so high. Our life in this town is difficult. There is no sleeping room for all of us here. I have slept a week on the floor in one of the houses, but I am compelled to leave even that floor because I do not have the money to pay for sleeping on it.

"I don't know where to go. I was born here and lived here all my life until the Germans came and sent me to the Oswiecim concentration camp. I have returned a short time ago. Nobody seems to want to help me because everyboby is having difficulties.

"I do wish the Americans came here to straighten out conditions. When are the Americans coming, do you know? We are all hungry. We get ration cards, but we just don't get the items listed on these cards."

The woman was bitterly disappointed when informed that the Americans, as far as we knew, had no plans of coming to Grodzisk.

She then pleaded to know when UNRRA would come to Grodzisk to distribute food and clothing. We advised her that UNRRA products had been turned over to the Polish government for distribution. She expressed hope that the distribution would take place soon so that the Polish people would get at least some bacon and fats, so sorely needed by the folk in her community.

Upon completing our lunch, which cost us approximately 180 zlotys, we went outside to our truck.

Scores of Grodzisk townsfolk, young and old, had gathered around our truck and stared at us. They closely scrutinized our tires, remarking about their high quality. They also looked over our clothes and commented on the quality as compared to the threadbare garb they wore. Although our lorry had the British flag painted clearly on the back and front, some Poles mistook it for the American flag, remarking to one another, "Amerykanski sztandar."

As our lorry driver started the motor and drove off, the Poles—children and adults alike—vigorously waved to us. Some, with tears in their eyes, shouted to us, "Come again, but don't forget to bring the bacon next time."

Our next stop was in Poznan, where we arrived in the darkness of night at 1 a.m., October 13. We stopped on the outskirts at the first Polish military station, requesting guidance to a hotel. A Polish soldier came out and accompanied us to it.

Poznan, called Posen by the Germans, in its architectural appearance, looks like a typical East German provincial city. It is, however, strongly Polish in flavor, custom and language. I was told that it was a city of 250,000 population before the war, but that now there were more than 325,000 persons crammed into the community despite the fact that at least 65% of the dwellings were damaged by bombings and severe fighting between Russians and the Germans.

The province of Poznan was the cradle of the Polish nation. In the province are the two earliest seats of the kingdom and the Catholic church in Poland. The first is Gniezno, which has been the residence of the Primate of Poland since the year 1000, and has a fine Gothic cathedral. The other is the city of Poznan itself, where the oldest rulers of the nation rest in hallowed tombs, and where a beautiful Renaissance town hall, a tenth century cathedral and a fine Baroque parish church of about 1700 stand out architecturally in the busy city.

We saw the severe war damage in Poznan, in the morning after we had our breakfast with Wladyslaw Wusza, economic adviser to the wojewoda Poznanski (provincial governor of Poznan). Wusza had greeted us at the hotel dining room. He explained to us the shortage of housing facilities in the greatly overpopulated city.

We found the cost of living in Poznan, as in Warsaw, extremely high. The Poles try their utmost to supplement their regular earnings by doing extra chores.

Russian troops garrison Poznan as is the case in other Polish communities. One Russian soldier, armed with a rifle, came out of the darkness at night near the hotel and seized a woman by the arm. A Polish soldier intervened, concocting a tale that the woman was brought to Poznan by British soldiers aboard our lorry, to visit relatives.

The Russian stalked off in anger.

Poznan restaurants stopped taking orders at 9 p.m. and closed their bars and premises at 10 p.m. There was an 11 p.m. curfew because of disturbances, such as robbery and looting, which occurred usually after that hour. A waiter explained that one night he was out in the street after 11 p.m., having been detained in his restaurant because of a wedding party, and was robbed of his clothes besides receiving a severe beating by a Russian soldier in uniform.

Poznan University was partly destroyed by British bombings during the German occupation, in an effort to drive out the Germans.

At the university, the roofs on some of the once splendid campus buildings were badly damaged. Some 3,000 students are crowded in whatever classrooms remain. Courses especially popular include languages (particularly English), medicine, law, economics, political science and business administration. Although there was room for only 360 medical students, more than 1,000 applications had been made.

Despite the severe destruction in Poznan, the city, as in pre-war days, is keeping its street clean.

Men were sweeping the autumn leaves. Their brooms were made of twigs tied to the end of a long pole. Piles of rubble—remains of Poznan buildings—still spilled over the sidewalks.

We visited St. Adalbert's Cemetery, where some of the most bitter fighting between the Germans and the Russians took place. At the rear of the cemetery was an ancient fortress, where the Germans held out for some time before finally retreating.

The tombstones and trees in the cemetery all bear scars of shells and machine gun bullets. In this cemetery are buried both German and Russian troops. In one corner are buried a British pilot shot down by the Germans in a night air raid and a British soldier who died while interned in Poland by the Germans.

Poznan was described as a political stronghold of Vice-Premier Stanislaw Mikolajczyk, leader of the Polish Peasant party, frowned upon by the Bierut regime.

A government official in Poznan stated that political positions throughout Poland were insecure. He said that security authorities had drawn up a list of names of persons who were prominent and politically active, other than those belonging to the Communist Polish Workers party. He stated that those on this list would be immediately arrested and held in the event of political disturbances in Poland as hostile to the provisional government.

In Poznan we met Dr. Oscar Lange, new Polish ambassador to the United States. Dr. Lange explained that he had been traveling for a number of days about Poland to learn about postwar conditions before going back to the United States. He complained that he had had considerable trouble with the Polish government automobile he had been traveling in. On one occasion, he said, the car broke down and his party was compelled to spend the night in a ditch.

Informed that the Poles had been complaining to us about the shortage of food and the distribution of UNRRA goods, Dr. Lange stated that as far as he knew the food rationing machinery in Poland had not been perfected.

Dr. Lange, professor of economics on leave from the University of Chicago, originally was a Polish subject, having been born in Poland. He was a professor at Cracow, and came to the United States shortly before the outbreak of World War II. He became a United States citizen in 1943.

Dr. Lange, who temporarily took the cloak of United States citizenship during the war, said that he did not renounce his United States citizenship but automatically lost it upon receiving a Polish passport. He said that he would not be in a position to discuss conditions he had noted on his tour of Poland until after he had presented his credentials to President Truman.

Following the brief chat with Dr. Lange and his secretary at breakfast in the Continental Hotel in Poznan, Williams, Lambert and I left the hotel to board our truck and resume our journey to Szczecin. Several hundred persons stood around the truck. All were talking excitedly and trying to guess what our nationality was and why we had come to Poznan.

Some of the curious Poles remarked that the American Red Cross must have come to feed and clothe them. Others presumed that an UNRRA truck had finally come to bring them fats, so badly needed by them. All were bitterly disappointed when they learned that we were neither Red Cross nor UNRRA officials, but merely newspapermen traveling through Poland. Many voices shouted, "Write truthfully about our present sufferings! Tell America to come to our aid with food and clothing!"

The Poles waved wildly to us as we drove off, although some were bitterly disappointed at receiving no aid from us.

On the outskirts of Poznan in the countryside we observed rich farmlands, where scores of Russian uniformed soldiers were harvesting potatoes. But as we drove on and on, we noticed vast expanses of once rich agricultural areas lying untilled and going to weed.

The countryside has been heavily fought over. Thousands of houses, especially in the former German territory farther west now belonging to Poland, are destroyed or partly destroyed. Sometimes we observed whole towns virtually razed and deserted.

The dwellings had been plundered and stripped by soldiers. Livestock, horses and cattle are gone. Machinery for the most part was missing also.

Into all this vast destruction and emptiness the Poles are being resettled.

Red and white Polish flags flutter from the partly damaged homes which the resettled Poles chose to live in. I have seen thousands of Poles, many in covered wagons and broken down trucks, coming along the rough roads from Old Poland to settle in the "new Promised Land," where they hoped to find greater opportunity for themselves and their children.

We asked the newly settled Poles why there were so many neglected large patches of potatoes. They told us that they had to secure permission of the Russian soldiers garrisoned in the vicinity before they could harvest any potatoes. This permission, the Poles told us, was granted only after the Russian troops had moved out.

Everywhere in the newly settled territory around Gorzow, which the Germans renamed Landsberg, were considerable signs of undercultivation of the land. Soil that clearly should have been plowed in September was still untouched. Much clover had gone to weed and where hay was gathered in often there were no barns to store it. There were no plows or farm implements. This was the picture all the way from Poznan to Gorzow.

Occasionally we drove through a village that was completely deserted except for a handful of old people, and some small children playing amid ruins. In some villages there were some undamaged homes but no one seemed to be living in them.

When we arrived in Gorzow, we had to make a detour around a beautiful bridge that the Germans had blown up as the Russian Army rapidly advanced toward the Warta River. I asked a Polish militiaman on traffic duty for directions to a restaurant and he volunteered to guide us to a good eating place. We crossed the Warta over a wooden bridge constructed by the Red Army. We invited the Polish militiaman, about 25, to be our guest at dinner. He readily accepted.

While eating, we had a lengthy interview with him. He said that he came from a small town near Czestochowa, having been inducted into the army last June. He added that the Poles in Gorzow were still experiencing difficulties with the Germans remaining in the community.

"Just this morning I arrested some Germans hiding in a basement of a bombed house. They had shot a Pole and were hiding there with his body."

The militiaman said that there were "only 20 Polish soldiers assigned to patrol duty in this town, while there are many Russian soldiers garrisoned here." He further explained that while he had a weapon, he was not provided with ammunition. He proved this to us by opening the weapon that resembled a "tommy gun."

Asked what his pay was, he said, "Forty-five zlotys (45c) a month; just enough for one bun." He thanked us profusely for the cigarets we handed him, explaining to us that he could not even buy a package of cigarets for his month's pay because "Polish cigarets cost 60 zlotys a package." We each also handed him from 50 to 100 zlotys. He was so elated that he jumped on our truck, after we finished eating, and led us out of town to the main highway leading toward Szczecin.

On the outskirts of Gorzow, the British soldiers stopped to pick up a Pole, who requested a "lift" to Mysliborz, formerly known as Soldin. The Pole jumped onto the rear of the truck, where Williams, Lambert and I had been sitting or lying on "jerry" gasoline cans throughout our journey. The Pole said he was a blacksmith, 55 years old, and that he had settled in this new Polish territory taken from the Germans just three months earlier. He came from Krakow.

"All is not as well in this new territory as we were told it would be before we settled here," he said. "We eat mostly potatoes and bread. Our earnings are small and the prices for food are extremely high. I and other skilled workers earn about 300 zlotys a week, which is little when you consider that I must pay some 400 zlotys a month for rent. I earned far more money in Krakow before coming here.

"I and other Poles left Krakow because of the intensive radio, newspaper and poster campaign promising 'new riches' to all settlers in this territory. Many farmers had also come with the city people to settle in the new area. Now many are returning because of the difficulties. All have become grossly disillusioned. The settlers came here in search of the 'nowe bogactwo' (new riches) promised by the government propaganda, but none of us found here anything but misery.

"Russian soldiers imprisoned in German camps were released in the summer and like a swarm of locusts swooped down on the farm of the new Polish settlers, taking away with them cattle, horses, farm implements and other necessities.

"The Polish settlers were unable to cope with the Russian bands and, consequently, were cleaned out. Despondently, thousands of new Polish settlers returned in poverty to communities from whence they came.

"The new Polish government promised us a 'paradise' in this new Polish land, but all we found was 'hell.' "

I asked him whether the Poles could complain to anyone about this Russian thievery.

"Yes, we could complain to the Russian Army garrison," said the Pole, "but the thieves would only be held in jail overnight. The next day, however, the Russian culprits would be released and in retaliation would make life even more miserable for us."

The Polish blacksmith stated that three German civilians work under him and the government has set their pay at about 4c for an eight hour day. These Germans supplemented their pay by carving novelties out of wood and selling them, according to the blacksmith.

"What are your living accommodations?" I asked the blacksmith.

"I live with my wife and four children in an old tenement building, divided into small family units," he said. "We pay far too much rent for the quarters. We have ration cards, but they are worthless. We subsist chiefly on potatoes and bread. The bread is very bad."

Shortly before we got to Mysliborz our truck stopped to pick up a young Polish woman, who wanted a "lift" to that town. She said she was 25 years old and had gone out into the country to buy some vegetables and other food "because the prices are much too high in Mysliborz." She had a small market basket containing a few eggs, carrots and potatoes. She said that she was repatriated from Germany, where she had worked as a maid for a German family. She said that the German Army seized her and other women near her home in Czestochowa during the war and sent her to Germany into forced labor. She said that after leaving Germany, the Russians stopped her in Gorzow and told her not to go farther, preventing her from returning to her home town.

"The Russians then assigned me to work in a candy factory," she related. "I am still working there. I receive six zlotys (6c) for each kilo of candy that I produce. If I work hard all day, I am able to earn 48 zlotys (48c) a day, but even that is far too little to purchase the necessary food and clothing that I need. I am staying over the week-end with friends at Mysliborz."

When we arrived at Mysliborz, which has a population of nearly 10,000, the Polish blacksmith and the woman candy factory worker jumped off the truck and bade us good-bye.

IX

TRACER BULLETS

Our entrance into Szczecin shortly before midnight was dramatic.

The driver of our British Army lorry had slowed down, feeling his way around the dark streets.

We heard intermittent shooting nearby. On several occasions, we saw bright red tracer bullets racing through the darkness enveloping the city's hideous ruins.

On the outskirts of the city were individual groups of civilians and Russian uniformed soldiers gathered around bonfires.

Our truck pushed on and on slowly into the heart of the city. We finally came to a lighted intersection and our lorry suddenly stopped. A group of hysterical Poles quickly surrounded us.

Our British Army major ordered his private to haul out his "tommy gun" to quiet the excited Poles, all of whom wanted to clamber onto our truck. The sight of the weapon quickly restored order.

"What seems to be the trouble?" the British major asked the Poles.

"One of our friends, a Polish militiaman, was wounded and we would like to have you take him to a hospital," answered one of the Poles, dressed in Polish Army uniform.

"Where is he?" asked the major.

"Not far from here, about a half block away," answered a young Polish woman, the only woman in the group of about 15.

The major agreed to take the wounded Polish militiaman to the hospital on condition that only the four he designated hop on the truck for the trip to the hospital. The group agreed, and the major designated the woman, the Polish uniformed soldier and two other Polish men to get into the truck. We then drove to the spot where the wounded militiaman lay near a curb and lifted him into the rear of the truck.

At the hospital admission was refused to the wounded militiaman. The Polish soldier then entered the hospital and insisted that emergency treatment be given to his friend because he was rapidly losing blood as he lay atop the gasoline "jerry" cans next to me. "What are hospitals for, if not to take care of people who are wounded and possibly dying?" remonstrated the Polish soldier.

The hospital authorities finally consented to admit the militiaman and he was carried out of the truck.

Naturally curious to know the circumstances of the shooting, we asked one of the Polish civilians aboard our truck to explain the incident.

"The militiaman was on duty to look after order in the city," explained the civilian, "when all of a sudden he heard this Polish woman, who is with us, scream. The militiaman walked up to her and asked what had happened. She explained that her purse was stolen by two Russian soldiers. As he was getting the details of this purse theft, the two Russian soldiers stepped up from behind a building and told him that it was none of his business as to what had happened.

"When the militiaman explained that it was his duty to maintain order and report such incidents as had happened, one of the Russian soldiers pulled out a revolver and shot the militiaman in his right thigh. The Russians then disappeared."

The Pole further explained that the Polish militiamen carried old French carbines that were unloaded, and furthermore, had orders not to prevent Russian soldiers from moving about as they pleased.

These militiamen do not have uniforms. Dressed in civilian garb, they wear red and white arm bands.

The Pole who explained the incident was in his early twenties. He said that he was captured during the war by the Germans with thousands of others serving in the Polish Youths' Army and was transferred to Germany, where he was confined in the Dachau concentration camp. He showed his wrist with a tattooed concentration camp number. He was sent by the Americans back to Poland following the defeat of the Germans. Subsequently, he resettled in Szczecin.

As this youthful Pole discussed the incident, he kept pulling out of his trouser leg a long hunting knife.

"I am going to kill the first Russian soldier I meet in the morning," he vowed in a hysterical tone of voice, "to avenge my dying comrade."

The youthful Pole said that he wished that the "real Polish Army would return to Poland."

"Not until the real Polish Army returns to Poland," he cried out, "will Poland be a free country, liberated from the Russians."

"What real Polish Army do you mean?" I asked him.

"The army of Gen. Wladyslaw Anders," he replied.

(Gen. Wladyslaw Anders, whose Polish troops based in Italy ousted the Germans from Monte Cassino in a bloody encounter, is despised by the Polish provisional government. The Bierut government in its new political dictionary for Polish soldiers charges Gen. Anders with "persecuting the democratic soldiers and officers and disgracefully leading out his Polish divisions to Persian deserts in a wasteful mission in the summer of 1942 during the German offensive against Stalingrad.")

Our truck now continued on to the city hall of Szczecin, where we wanted to meet the mayor in an effort to get hotel accommodations.

While en route to the city hall, we got lost in the ghastly, terrifying ruins of the dark city. We heard repeated shots fired and when two tracer bullets crossed the path of our truck, we really shuddered. Williams, Lambert, and I hugged the floor of the truck, hiding behind the "jerry" cans for safety, for the shots were much too close for comfort. But the lorry kept going.

After driving around for about a half hour, which to us seemed like several long hours, we finally found the city hall. Much to our distress, however, the mayor of Szczecin was not in his office. He had left the city for Warsaw earlier that day. The only one whom we found on duty was a young lieutenant in a Polish Army uniform. I spoke to him in Polish, requesting his assistance in procuring us accommodations at the Continental Hotel. His reply in Polish clearly indicated that he was not a Pole, but a Russian. His pronunciation and the Russian newspapers on his desk were ample proof.

The lieutenant directed a young Polish militiaman to help direct us to the hotel, but since this militiaman came to Szczecin only three days ago, he had some difficulties in locating it. We drove around and around for an hour among the city's ruins before we finally came upon the hotel.

The following morning and the next few days we had a glimpse in Szczecin of the greatest migration of peoples in its history.

We saw thousands of Poles brought to Szczecin from a British displaced persons camp in Germany, while thousands of Germans were heading westward. The first 1,000 to arrive in Szczecin came on Sunday, Oct. 14, 1945. I was the only American to observe these Poles alight from the convoy of 35 British Army trucks. These Poles entered the repatriation barracks, where they remained for 24 hours until they were catalogued and assigned to trains leaving for "inside" Poland, including points in the former German area east of the Oder.

On Monday, October 15, and Tuesday, October 16, two more convoys brought 6,000 additional Poles of all ages from Germany. British Army authorities said that some 500,000 Poles, under their jurisdiction in Germany, were to be repatriated throughout the fall, winter and spring. All were to be brought to the repatriation depot in Szczecin, where British responsibility involving the displaced Poles ceased. The British provided each Pole with rations for nine days, enough until the Poles arrived at their final destination.

The repatriated Poles brought their meager possessions in potato sacks, wicker baskets, baby buggies, coaster wagons of ancient vintage and blankets. All were tired from the long journey, but appeared happy to be returned to their "fatherland" after years of wandering and hard labor in concentration camps.

Some 20 Polish Army officers, interned in Germany after the unsuccessful Warsaw insurrection, were among the first group of 1,000 repatriates.

"I feel sorry for those officers," a Polish woman who works at the repatriation depot said.

"Why?" I inquired.

"Because any soldier who participated against the Germans in the Warsaw insurrection is looked upon with great disfavor by the Warsaw government," she said. "These officers will find life difficult in Poland. They would be much better off if they had not returned to Poland."

The first group of 1,000 Polish repatriates were unloaded from the trucks and assigned to dormitories within 20 minutes, so well were the details for their arrival worked out by Alex Nasielski, director of the repatriation project at Szczecin. The dormitories were inside long buildings, once used by the Germans as public institutions, for the blind, hard of hearing and the aged.

The returning Poles were largely deported by the German Army to be used as slave laborers. Many of them now were seeing Poland for the first time in years. Some of the children, however, had never seen Poland until now.

Nasielski and his crew of assistants hurriedly served hot coffee—very black and without milk—to the repatriates immediately upon their arrival at the repatriation depot.

In addition to this depot, I visited in Szczecin another center, this one for Poles arriving from the east to settle in the new Oder River area, formerly German ruled.

This second center had been in operation only a week, according to Nasielski. And yet in that brief period some

42,000 Poles, from Krakow, Warsaw, Lublin and other eastern cities had been registered and passed through to acquire "homesteads" in the battle scarred Oder River area, where only a few months earlier bitter war had raged between the German, Polish and Russian armies.

This so-called "Etap Nr. 1" (Stage No. 1) was formerly a German high school of excellent construction. A number of German men were working in the stables and cleaning up the courtyard. German women were in the huge kitchen cleaning the six huge food vats in which coffee and soup were made for distribution among the Polish arrivals from the east.

Hundreds of Polish women were sitting around in their dormitories and chatting, while their barefooted youngsters ran around in carefree play. These women were waiting to be transferred to the new areas and were looking forward to settling down after months of wandering.

All Poles arriving at the two centers took a bath upon admittance and had their clothes disinfected.

"The sick are isolated from the physically fit," said Nasielski, "and placed in infirmaries. A medical staff, consisting of a doctor and a nurse at each depot, is on hand to treat the ill. Medical supplies are not in abundance, but we do our best with what we have. The doctor especially looks out for Poles with asthma because asthmatic persons will not find the Oder River region suitable to live in. Those with asthma, therefore, are sent back to the Polish districts from which they came."

One newspaper, *Kurier Sczcecinski*, is being published daily in Szczecin. On Sunday, October 14, 1945, when the first repatriated Poles from the British zone arrived, this newspaper carried a lengthy editorial greeting the "repatriates" back to their homeland.

In Szczecin each day were lines of German war prisoners still wearing their army uniforms. These columns of former "supermen" were being led by Polish militiamen to work projects in the area to clean up the debris or tear down gutted buildings. These once proud, cocky Germans appeared broken down and sullen.

Many Poles stated in Szczecin that the elderly German men and women for the most part were co-operative in doing menial work, but that some of the younger element, particularly boys 12 to 16 years old, were defiant and brazenly wore the Nazi insignia on their caps. Some of these German youths occasionally remarked to the Polish boys, "Just wait, this won't last long. There will come a day when you will be sorry." Although there were many more Germans still living in Szczecin in the fall of 1945 than Poles, no serious clashes between them had occurred.

Nasielski and other officials at Szczecin refer to it as the "Klondike" of the new Poland.

Szczecin under Germany housed 300,000 persons, mostly Germans. About 40,000 resettled Poles and some 60,000 Germans, all of whom were eventually to be removed, lived in Szczecin in the fall of 1945. Ultimately, some 200,000 Poles are expected to live in this city.

Before World War II, Szczecin was a beautiful, well laid-out city, with many boulevards and tree-flanked promenades. The town suffered its severest damage from American bombing raids, which destroyed from 70% to 80% of the buildings and warehouses in the harbor district. Some 120,000 German civilians are reported to have lost their lives in Szczecin during the war. About

75% of the Falkenwald, the exclusive residential district with modern villas and gardens, remained intact or has been restored and now is occupied by the new Polish settlers. The blocks and blocks of factories, including automobile, sugar, cement and paper plants, were for the most part destroyed and the surviving machinery taken away by the Russian Army.

The area of Szczecin is bigger than Warsaw's. Under the treaty of Versailles, it was a free port for Czecho-Slovakia, allowing the Czechs to bring up their exports there along the Oder River. In 1937 Hitler denounced the treaty and the Czechs no longer used the port. While on a tour of the city, I observed Russians in the harbor area stripping equipment and making it ready for shipment to Russia. A Polish soldier explained that the Russians were allowed a certain percentage of materials from Szczecin, but that "no one checks up on how much the Russians are actually taking out because no one may enter the harbor area proper." The Russians could be seen crating machinery and heavy materials through the wire fence surrounding the harbor area.

Russian troops are stationed all over Szczecin. Quite often they marched in long columns down the streets of the city. When marching, they generally sing.

Many Poles whom I met in Szczecin spoke in whispers and lived in fear of the Russians. Several said that the Russians kill about 50 Poles a week here. Some of the killings take place in broad daylight on the streets, in the black market and amid the ruins of the city. There were also frequent assaults and robberies committed by the Russians upon the Poles. Storekeepers said that their stocks were looted and their homes entered and ransacked at all hours of the day and night. The Russians even entered the Polish settlers' center and committed acts of vandalism.

Szczecin had very limited street illumination in the fall of 1945, and as a result the newly arrived Polish settlers were afraid to venture out into the streets because of the roving Russian soldiers, who would attack, rob and even shoot them.

In the two-block-long black market in Szczecin were a number of Germans selling their wares before moving into the city.

Authorities said that occasionally a shooting occurs in this black market. I was convinced that such incidents do occur, for while being in a book store across the street from the black market, I heard a shot fired. The Polish woman clerk cried, "O, Boze, znowu strzelaja!" (Oh, God, they are shooting again!) People in the black market screamed and ran. I looked out the window and noticed a great confusion.

The aftermath of war is truly terrifying, shocking and bewildering. Americans who have not seen a city—as big as Milwaukee or Buffalo—changing from the jurisdiction of one country to another would find such change a great adventure.

For example, newly settled Poles in Szczecin were taking over stores that formerly belonged to the Germans.

The Poles were changing the signs on the German stores reading "Markthalle," "Fleischerei," "Metzgerei," or "Apotheke," to their Polish equivalents. The Poles decorated each store entrance with a Polish red and white flag in place of the hated swastika. In a number of the stores the Poles were telling the Germans to wipe the dust off the counters and to mop the floors.

Three Polish banks have been established in Szczecin in the fall of 1945, but I did not observe any doing a "rush business" for the Poles are as poor as the proverbial church mice.

In the closing hours of our stay in Szczecin, we saw hundreds of Germans leaving their beloved city. Many of them were old and feeble. Many others were tiny tots clinging to their mothers—the fathers having gone off to war never to return. One young woman was holding a boy and girl in each hand. Around her neck was tied a blanket with an infant dangling in it in front of her, while on her back she carried a potato sack filled with her family's possessions. She wandered aimlessly down the battle-torn highway toward an unknown destination.

*   *   *

The area which this German woman and her three youngsters were leaving became the subject of a heated international controversy months after I left Poland, when Secretary of State Byrnes on September 6, 1946, in a speech at Stuttgart, Germany, rejected the idea that Germany's eastern borders were fixed permanently on the Oder River.

Byrnes stated at Stuttgart that the frontiers of Poland in the west were only provisionally agreed to at Potsdam, that no exact territorial settlement was made, and that final settlement was to be part of the general peace settlement in Europe.

Russia and its puppet Polish provisional government in Warsaw immediately challenged Byrnes's statement on the grounds that the "United States, Britain and Russia already are committed to fixing Poland's western border along the Oder River because they accepted the evacuation of 2,000,000 Germans from the territory taken over by the Poles."

In a bristling counterstatement, Soviet Foreign Minister V. M. Molotov declared that the Potsdam agreement already had "determined the western Polish frontiers (along the Oder and western Neisse rivers), and it is only awaiting now the formal confirmation at the future international conference for drafting the peace treaty with Germany."

"Who would have thought that this evacuation of Germans might have been considered as a temporary experiment?" Molotov inquired.

In Poland the Communist newspaper *Glos Ludu* stated that Byrnes's speech meant only that "he wanted to rebuild a great and powerful Germany." The editorial further stated:

"Poland will not discuss the subject of the western lands. We took them over and we shall not leave them. Poland is an independent country. American reaction may dictate its will on the Philippines and the Hawaiian Islands. In Poland it will not dictate and will not force anything on us. The Soviet Union, whose forces stand west of the Oder, completely shares our attitude."

Byrnes's statement at Stuttgart and the repercussions growing out of it is another illustration tending to show why Poland remains "a keg of dynamite" in Europe.

Poland, which is steadily expelling Germans from the Oder River territory and resettling 4,000,000 Poles in this western section, is just as bewildered about the agreements made at Potsdam as the rest of the world outside of Russia's iron curtain.

The 4,000,000 Poles have practically been "dumped" into this area, for many of them were resettled without their consent. Human rights to a large extent have been disregarded entirely by Polish and Russian officials responsible for this vast migration. Russia was keenly anxious that this Oder River territory be filled quickly by Poles against possible future German claims to this land.

The Poles, who aimlessly wandered with their skimpy belongings in this war-scarred territory in search of shelter in the form of shell-torn or bombed dwellings formerly occupied by German families, faced an uncertain, miserable life, for they had neither materials nor tools with which to rebuild their "new homesteads."

POLAND'S HORSES HEADING EAST TO RUSSIA

X

WHISPERING PEASANTS

Curious to know how a large landowner's estate looks, how the peasants fared through the German occupation and what the present status of the estate appears, Williams, Lambert and I made arrangements with the British soldiers driving the lorry to take us to a typical estate on the journey back from Szczecin to Warsaw.

The British lorry almost went off the road into a culvert as it churned its way along knee-deep mud toward a small Polish village, which I designated simply as Village K for "security" reasons. This village was a typical large landowner's estate.

Six years of warfare and neglect of road construction and repair have left most of the roads and highways in extremely bad condition. But this narrow, winding, muddy road was the worst of all that we had encountered during the week's travel aboard the British truck.

As the truck finally pulled into the estate grounds— some 20 miles east of Poznan, excited lean men and women came running out of their huts. Also several dozen children who had been playing suddenly screamed with fright when we hopped out of the truck. Later, it was explained to us, that the children thought we were new invaders. The old folks said in Polish that the children had gone through so much misery during the German occupation of the estate, and later under the Russian occupation, that they were fearful that they might have to undergo a similar ordeal with our arrival.

The children beamed and came close to us when the old folks explained to them that we were friends. I dug into my pocket and distributed sticks of gum that I had brought with me from the United States for just such an occasion. The little tots curiously unwrapped the sticks of gum; several of them bit off the gum piece by piece and swallowed it like candy. One little girl did not unwrap her stick of gum. Instead, she put it into her dress pocket and occasionally pulled it out to sniff the spearmint aroma.

Our right rear tire sustained a "flat" as we were driving into the estate grounds. While the British private was changing the tire, the peasant children watched his every move. They giggled as the jack raised the rear end of the lorry.

Some 95 peasant families, comprising about 800 persons, were found living on this 3,000-acre estate. The owner went to America for a visit in June, 1939, but never returned because of the German invasion, I was told by the village blacksmith.

The landowner's mother—a grand old lady of 76—remained living in the landowner's 20-room house that looks like a castle, until the Germans came and drove her out in the fall of 1939. She fled to some friends near Warsaw, returning only recently to be cared for by the peasants who had worked for her family for years.

"How did the Germans treat you all here when they took over this property?" I asked the village blacksmith, who acted as spokesman for the peasants.

"Life was terrible for us here," he said. "The Germans would shoot anyone for failure to comply with an order promptly. They had us all working hard on the farm. We got little to eat from them. The Germans took about 25 of our people and sent them away. We have heard from only five so far.

"Then when the Russians advanced, the Germans fled quickly without taking any of the livestock. But when the Russians left some months ago, they took away the 50 horses and 150 cows that we had. Furthermore, the Russians ruined all of the furniture and took everything they could carry out of the landowner's house."

The village blacksmith took Williams, Lambert and me to the landowner's house to show the extensive damage which he said the Russians had done.

We saw windows that were broken, plumbing smashed to bits, light fixtures battered and the few remaining pieces of furniture chopped up. We noticed some fir-tree branches hanging above some of the doors, and the blacksmith explained, "Oh, those branches were from a Christmas celebration before the war."

I asked the blacksmith about the new land reform program and how it affected his village.

"The government has divided 1,500 acres of the estate's land among us peasants," he said, "while the remaining 1,500 acres are being supervised by a public-land administrator. It is still too early for us to say just how things will work out here under the land-reform program. What we need most right now is livestock, horses and cattle."

On the basis of dividing 1,500 acres among 95 families in this village, each peasant family would have received approximately 16 acres of land under the land-reform program.

I closely scrutinized the clothes of the peasants and found them to be ragged. Many of the peasants were in bare feet. The shoes worn by the others were all hand made and old. The aged mother of the landowner is dependent on the charity of the peasants she once ruled with her son.

"She is old and we certainly cannot turn her away," said one woman peasant. "Where would she go? As long as we have anything to eat, we will share it with her. She came to us as the last resort for assistance. We know she had no right to be here, but after all she is as human as we are."

The aged mother of the landowner told us she went through many hardships since being driven out of her son's beautiful, three-story manor house. She had not eaten anything for days at a time. She returned to the village after the war's end, frail and haggard and without shoes. The peasants greeted her with tears in their eyes and hurriedly made a pair of shoes for her.

The row of peasant huts stood in sharp contrast to the landowner's fine, white brick and frame mansion. These peasants' huts were frail and small. The floors were either of a thin layer of cement or hard clay. The peasant's sanitation facilities were near nil, and their furniture was homemade. The beds had no mattresses. The peasants slept on heaps of straw with worn-out sheets over it.

The peasants in Village K were as perplexed about their future as was the aged mother of the landowner living in American exile.

It was still too early for them to have any opinion about the land reform. They had not fully recovered from the effects of nearly six years of German occupation and were still talking about their ordeals in whispers.

One aged Polish woman, who reminded me in her appearance of the many Polish women in the thickly-populated Fourteenth Ward in Milwaukee, told me: "You cannot talk much even today about conditions for fear of arrest. We are not happy with life as it is today. The war is over, but there is still much misery. Russian soldiers often stop here and rob us of food."

After spending several hours with the peasants in Village K, we hopped into the lorry and proceeded on our journey to Lodz.

As a result of the destruction wrought by the Germans in Warsaw, Lodz has become now the largest city in Poland.

Latest figures in the fall of 1945 showed that the population of Lodz—the textile center of Poland—was 460,000 as compared to about 400,000 in devastated Warsaw. Before the war Lodz had a population of 550,000.

"Our population in Lodz dropped considerably because the Germans murdered 200,000 Jews," said Stefan Lucinski, director of the Polish Chamber of Commerce. "Only 9,000 Jews were spared."

Asked for a brief background of Lodz, Lucinski said: "Lodz is a comparatively young city, only 120 years old. The Jews in the city lived in various sections until the Germans came and centralized them all in a ghetto. The Germans then methodically liquidated them.

"There was no fighting in Lodz between the Germans and the Russians. Consequently, the city is scarcely damaged by the war, although the Germans burned about 20% of the homes in the ghetto they had established.

"The Germans fled from Lodz on January 17, 1945. About 80% of the large factories here were in production during the German occupation, while the small factories were looted and the machinery taken to Germany. The Germans chiefly produced rayon during the occupation, paying the Poles small wages.

"In their flight from the city, the Germans did not have sufficient time to loot all of the factories. They looted only about 20% of the machinery."

After leaving Lodz, our lorry proceeded back to Warsaw. On this final lap of our week-long journey deep into the Polish hinterland we had taken along with us a woman passenger, who requested a "lift" to the Polish capital. She stated that she was without funds and was going to Warsaw to take up some matter with the Polish government.

As our truck rumbled along, this woman talked much about her suffering the last six years. She was 38 years old, but she appeared more like 50 because of the ordeal she had undergone. She expressed a burning hatred for the Germans.

"Never in my life have I had the courage to kill a chicken," she said. "Even now I could not do it. But I have such a hatred against the Germans for what they have done to the Poles and to me that I would not hesitate to kill a German if I had the opportunity.

"My husband was a druggist before the German occupation. He had a nice business in Warsaw and we had a beautiful villa on the outskirts. When the Germans came, they began shooting the Poles at random on the streets. They plundered whatever they wanted. They chased my husband out of his store. They also took over our villa, and my husband and I went to live with some friends in an old Warsaw house.

"One day my husband was out walking on a Warsaw street and the Germans seized him. They put him on a truck and drove away. I have never heard from him again."

Apolonia wept as she told her story. My eyes glistened, too.

"Then, when the insurrection took place," said Apolonia, wiping her tears with a tiny, worn-out handkerchief, "all hell seemed to break loose. They poked fun at our priests, as they marched them out of their rectories. Some of the German soldiers put on the priestly clothes of the Holy Mass, while others paraded carrying crucifixes, and all went through profane antics. I saw German soldiers throw grenades and incendiary bombs into the churches to blow them to pieces. The towers crashed with thunderous echo. I saw St. Alexander's Church go to pieces.

"We Poles all fled out of the city from the horrible sights and hid in the ditches along the highways and in the fields. There were piercing horrible screams as frightened horses and cattle began rampaging over the fields where we had hidden. The stampede was caused by the fires and detonations in nearby Warsaw, where the Germans methodically were exploding to bits building after building in revenge for the insurrection.

"The horses and cattle ran over many of the Poles who had sought shelter in the fields. I was especially sorry for the children who trembled under the protective bodies of their mothers, grandmothers and grandfathers."

Apolonia said that she was kicked by a horse on her right cheek and pointed to a scar that stretched from her eye to the middle of the cheek.

"Now do you wonder," she said, "why I hate the Germans as I do? I don't believe that any American can fully realize the extreme suffering and persecution that the

Poles experienced under German occupation. What I don't understand is why the Poles in America didn't kill some Germans there in revenge for our suffering."

When I explained to her that in America the people are not differentiated by nationalities and that all of the people in the United States regard each other as Americans, Apolonia blinked in bewilderment and said:

"That's the way I would like to live in peace and harmony, without having any one question me whether I was a Pole or persecute me because I was a Pole. Isn't there any chance for me to get to America?"

I advised Apolonia that her only chance of getting to America would be through the proper immigration procedure.

I then asked Apolonia why she wanted to leave Poland now that the Germans were defeated and were gone from her country. Apolonia cried out, "We still are not free. We do not have our own government. The government operating in Poland now was set up by Moscow and favors only Communists."

XI

GHOST TOWNS AND FORBIDDEN ZONES

Transportation and roads leading to Gdynia were in extremely bad condition when I traveled to the Polish "miracle port" on the Baltic Sea with an American Army truck convoy, which was sent to Gdynia to bring supplies from a Victory ship for the American embassy in Warsaw. The American soldiers driving in the convoy had come to Poland from Berlin, with other supplies for the embassy. Their assignment to pick up additional supplies for the embassy from the Gdynia port afforded me another opportunity to travel into another section of the Polish hinterland.

There were many fascinating sights along Gdynia's waterfront—the aftermath of nearly six years of war.

For example, the German battleship, *Schleswig-Holstein*, which, it is claimed, fired the first shots of World War II, lay sunk at a Gdynia dock as a result of American and British bombing. The big battleship has been stripped of all her guns. She sank along with 20 other German ships struck by Allied bombs. The Poles on guard duty at the port told me that about 100 Germans lost their lives in the sinking of the *Schleswig-Holstein*.

At the entrance of the inner basin was the 7,000-ton radio-driven ship, *Zwilligen*, which the Germans scuttled in an attempt to block the basin. UNRRA vessels in the fall of 1945 were able to pass through, however.

121

Partly blocking the outer basin of Gdynia Harbor, where the sea walls were blown by the Germans, lay the *Gneisenau*, 26,000-ton German battleship.

The *Gneisenau* was the famous craft that defied the British Navy in the run to Brest during the war. It had been stripped of its guns, but was still covered with its camouflaged netting. The ship was scuttled by the Germans after being damaged by Allied bombings.

Only a few electric cranes remain in operation in Gdynia. Many others had been destroyed or damaged by German demolition or Allied bombing. Most of the warehouses likewise had been destroyed.

The Poles in Gdynia operated many stores already in the fall of 1945, and while expensive fur coats and other luxury items, including jewelry, were being sold, there was an acute shortage of everyday clothing for sale in the stores.

On the outskirts of Gdynia were two vast "graveyards" of German tanks, self-propelled guns, half-tracks, anti-aircraft guns and other abandoned and "knocked-out" war equipment, German as well as Russian.

Gdynia—known as the "miracle port" prior to the outbreak of World War II—is part of a coast line of about 50 miles which Poland received at the end of the first World War. It is located at the tip of a narrow strip of land referred to by the Germans prior to the last war as "The Polish Corridor." In 1918 Gdynia was only a small fishing village with only 56 inhabitants and no railway communications.

Within 15 years it became a city of 120,000 inhabitants and the new port became the most important trade center on the Baltic Sea. The Poles regarded this enterprise as a proof of Polish energy, initiative and abilities. Hence, they referred to Gdynia as the "miracle port."

Most of the city of Gdynia was standing undamaged at the close of the war, although in the harbor area cranes and warehouses and most of the piers were either demolished completely or badly damaged. The modernistic white business and apartment buildings—the pride of the short-lived Polish republic resurrected in 1918—still rose majestically undamaged in the fall of 1945.

Between Gdynia and Gdansk is Sopot, which was known under German occupation as Zoppot. The big white casino, where the German soldiers relaxed by gambling during the occupation of Poland, is completely destroyed as a result of warfare. The Poles in Sopot said that this resort town, commonly referred to as the "Atlantic City of Poland," was heavily mined by the Germans to balk the Russian advance in that area.

Gdansk—known until September 1, 1939, as the Free City of Danzig—was referred to in the fall of 1945 by the new Polish settlers as the "Little City of Warsaw" because of the extensive damage there patterned after the destruction of the Polish capital.

German workers, chiefly women, were cleaning up the rubble under supervision of the Poles, who run the port city of Danzig since the fall of 1945. The city and harbor had been laid low by artillery and demolitions, although limited street car service was in operation and extremely slow trains are running into a battered station.

Germans at a market square in Danzig were selling their possessions before departing to some undetermined destination in the West. They complained bitterly about being forced to move.

Most of the Poles who took over the Gdansk homes and business shops of former Germans came from Wilno, now in Russian hands. The newly settled Poles complained that they had to leave their beloved Wilno. One said, "It just cannot be that I must not return to my Wilno. It just isn't right."

Gdansk was a prosperous Polish port for centuries. Prussia seized it in the second partition of Poland in 1793. It became a free city under League-of-Nations control after World War I. Hitler seized it in 1939.

In one section of the city still stand gas and oil tanks camouflaged by the German Army to conceal them from Allied bombers. Russian soldiers were busy in the Gdansk harbor, as they were in the Szczecin harbor, salvaging whatever they could for shipment to Russia.

A tour through East Prussia disclosed a long series of "ghost towns," which the Germans abandoned in their flight before the advancing Russians. Some of these small towns had scores of homes. Yet not a single person was seen in them. There were only a few persons in Tannenberg, where the Hindenburg monument, dedicated to the Germans' victory over the Russians on August 14, 1914, still stands undamaged.

East Prussian towns, which are being taken over by newly settled Poles, reminded the traveler of the "ghost towns" of America's "Wild West" of another era. Even the farmlands were unoccupied. Neither man nor beast could be seen for miles around. The abandonment was as complete as in many sections in the newly Polish-acquired Oder River area.

"Where to?" was a frequent question voiced by Germans leaving the "ghost towns" in East Prussia.

"Where to?" was also a frequent question voiced by Poles seeking new homes upon their arrival in the "ghost towns" from their age-old homes east of the Curzon line.

With the acquisition of 40,000 square miles, part of it former Polish soil, from Germany, Poland in the fall of 1945 had a total of 250 additional miles of coastline. But visitors were strictly prohibited by the Russians from traveling through most sections of the area along the seacoast, especially the territory extending from Gdynia to Szczecin. A Polish soldier said that "no one may enter the hundreds of miles of newly-acquired Polish territory from Germany along the coast because the Russian Army was operating there." Consequently, neither the Poles nor the rest of the outside world know what is going on in those areas.

Searching for Coal

XII

VIGNETTES FROM BEHIND THE IRON CURTAIN

Blacked out from the rest of the civilized world by Hitler for nearly six years and now veiled by Stalin's iron curtain, Poland is a war-weary country with many personal tragedies and heart-breaking scenes, some of which I have particularly noted in my travels through the Polish hinterland in the fall of 1945 and herewith present as vignettes from behind the iron curtain. Included are a variety of anecdotes that will prove of interest to Americans curious about the predicament of life in post-war Poland.

WARSAW

In this war battered city, as in all other Polish communities, Polish troops under direction of Red Army officers set up loud speakers at important thoroughfares in the fall of 1945. The loud speakers blared incessant Communist propaganda urging the Poles to support the Soviet established Polish puppet government and to join the Communist Polish Workers party.

* * *

A pretty Polish girl, about 16, entered a Warsaw restaurant selling toothbrushes. Her left leg was missing. She moved around with the aid of one crutch. The girl wept with joy when Larry Allen, Associated Press correspondent, and I each handed her 50 zlotys without asking for the toothbrush.

"You are so kind," said the girl. "May God bless you."

She turned around and went out the door into the hideous ruins of Warsaw.

* * *

While driving into Warsaw following a trip to Gdynia, I observed an aged woman, perhaps in her seventies, sitting at a small bonfire on the first floor of a ghostlike, gutted-out seven-story building. The old woman had a blanket wrapped around her head. A rosary dangled from her hands, which were slightly outstretched to be warmed by the fire. Pedestrians walked by without taking any notice of the poor, old woman. Truly pitiful is the state of life in the once proud Polish capital!

* * *

Early risers in the Polonia Hotel do not need alarm clocks to wake them up in the morning. Street hawkers are out early in front of the hotel and do a splendid job in rousing even the soundest sleepers. These street hawkers are boys and old men and women. They sell chiefly cigarets, newspapers and new Polish maps. They shout their wares—"Papierosy!" (Cigarets); "Gazety!" (Newspapers), and "Nowe Polskie Mapy!" (New Polish Maps)—incessantly from 6 a.m. to 10 p.m. each day.

* * *

The saddest day in Poland in the fall of 1945 was November 1, designated by the Polish provisional government as "Memorial Day." It was a legal holiday. The people went to church in the morning, for it was also

"All Saints' Day"—a holy day of obligation. After the church services, the people went to cemeteries, where they decorated the graves of their loved ones who died in action or were murdered by the Germans or Russians. Thousands of Poles in Warsaw also prayed at the little shrines set up in front of their gutted homes. Candles burned throughout the night and little memorial flags at these shrines fluttered in the autumn breeze. Small Red Cross girls, 8 to 13 years of age, conducted hourly vigils in front of municipal shrines, where the Germans had killed Poles in groups varying up to 100. These shrines are erected on bullet-riddled walls of buildings. A long, mournful procession leading through Warsaw streets to the grave of the unknown soldier was held on the afternoon of November 1. The period of mourning continued through the following day, which the people observed as "All Souls' Day."

* * *

Young, attractive women—18 to 25—are the traffic cops in Warsaw and other Polish cities. They wear Polish Army uniforms with white cuffs on their outer sleeves. They are very stern in directing traffic and fire a salvo of hot words at an erring Polish motorist. When an American car is coming toward their intersection, they immediately give it the right of way and occasionally wink at the handsome American soldier chauffeur. Young women, clad in Polish Army uniforms, also serve as conductors on streetcars.

* * *

A curious laboratory is operated at 12 Chmielna Street in the Polish capital by Wladyslaw Woyton, who calls his "invention" Woyton's Rays. One day Woyton, who is in his seventies and sports a gray beard, told me: "My rays produce a regenerative reconstruction of cells of the human body and, hence, of all kinds of tissues, including those of which bone, tendons, muscles and nerves are made up. The possibilities of the invention are not limited to curing the wounded. About 120,000,000 sufferers from rheumatism and arthritis await relief; so do millions of people suffering from diseases of the heart, kidneys, liver, asthma, general debility, exhaustion and impaired eyesight. The apparatus may be turned out in several box-type models of varied kilowatt strength." Woyton promised me great financial success if I would peddle his "invention" in America for him.

* * *

Thirty-six American soldiers live here in a white cement block home that was formerly the living quarters of a Polish nobleman. The site is a spot in the woods some 14 miles from devastated Warsaw. The GI's are chauffeurs, mechanics, supplymen and, if an emergency arises, they also serve as guards for the United States embassy. I found them to be extremely homesick in this faraway outpost, and some of them expressed a great desire to return to America. Their chief complaints were lack of recreational facilities in battered Warsaw and the curfew at midnight imposed for "safety reasons" growing out of the nightly shootings. A radio station is maintained here for contact with the United States Army at Frankfurt, Germany.

* * *

The Polish provisional government decreed a new marriage law for Poland. It provides for the civil registration of all marriages. Religious marriages are admissible but not obligatory. Persons from 18 years up may marry. They must present a medical certificate. Certain diseases disqualify a person for marriage. Important reasons have to be given for divorce, although if one spouse is German, the other may obtain a divorce for that reason.

* * *

United States money is the most sought currency in Poland. I saw a black market dealer in money sell English pound notes in the Polonia Hotel for American money at the rate of one pound for $2.50. In England one pound notes at the time were being exchanged at the rate of $4.10. Americans leaving for England bought a sizable amount of the pound notes in Warsaw. The Polish zlotys have no recognized foreign exchange value, being honored only within the boundaries of Poland. The only official rate recognized by the Polish provisional government is 100 zlotys for an American dollar, but black market operators eager to get hold of American dollars give as much as 310 zlotys for one dollar. If the right contact was made in the Lodz black market, one could get as much as 12,000 zlotys for an American $10 bill.

* * *

The Communist journalists delight in writing satirical articles in the Polish press about visiting foreigners, particularly Americans and Englishmen, and at the same time praise to high heaven the conduct of the Russians in Poland. Here is a sample satire entitled "The Warsaw Mail Coach" written by Marian Podkowinski for the *Dziennik Polski* (governmental "Polish Daily"):

"When some English general arrived before the war, all the newspapers just gurgled with joy and pride. And here, if you please, is an English general walking down the Avenue, and not just any general—for he is from the Royal Guard, those who wear busbys and hold guard before Buckingham Palace—and nobody even pays any attention to him. He is over six feet tall, in gala dress; he looks as if he had come out of *Harper's Magazine*. But he is not an exception. We have here numerous English, American, French officers, without mentioning, of course, Soviet officers, whom we treat as friends.

"If anybody attracts the attention of the crowd, it may be that little Scot in his Tartan Kilt, who accompanies the general on his morning escapades. Besides army men, we have an innumerable number of civilians from various countries of Europe and America. The 'Polonia' and the 'Central' hotels are simply swarming with foreigners, so that walking about their halls, you forget your own language on the way.

"Do not let us wonder that so many of them are coming to see us now. After all, for these Americans, bored with the quiet and exaggeratedly simplified life in normal towns on the other side of the ocean, the stay in Warsaw is a fairy tale, a new thrill of unknown adventures; it is exoticism, novelty, madness. And in truth those Americans rant, just as in Hollywood films.

"They laugh, chew gum, make a noise and as for their dancing, it is quite impossible. Sometimes one has the impression of watching a Laurel-and-Hardy film.

"Much was said in Poland about the behavior of the Russians in bars. But from my experience, I must state that Russian officers behave with quite greater moderation —I should say with even greater reserve."

The Communist journalists in their articles published in the Polish government press strive to tear down the respect the general Polish public has for the Americans and the British, but the Americans and British continue to be popular among the people wherever they travel in the Polish hinterland while the Russians are frowned upon.

* * *

One Sunday night while eating at the Polonia Hotel dining room, I observed a Russian officer in a heated argument with a Pole in the lobby. The Russian appeared under the influence of vodka, which is the common spirit sold here. I saw the Russian punch his adversary who dropped to the floor. Hotel employees rushed about to quell the disturbance.

* * *

Warsaw's first postwar business directory was issued in the fall of 1945. It consisted of 36 pages listing private and public institutions and bureaus and 8 pages of advertising. It was called *"Informator."* The publishers stated that great difficulties were encountered in compiling the first directory due to the ruins of Warsaw and ex- pressed assurance that the next issue would be more complete. The bureau of statistics of the Republic of Poland also issued at the same time its first postwar issue of *"Statistical News."* An editorial note stated: "The restored *Statistical News* are intended to be a con- tinuation of pre-war *News.* It is evident, however, that different conditions and new forms of economic and social life had to modify its contents."

* * *

The Polish press on October 15, 1945 disclosed that two parasites had been brought into Poland by the UNRRA. One was described as a bug which feeds on leguminous plants and the other as a Brazilian grain bug. They were further described as "very harmful and dangerous." The government declared that "in case their presence is established on any foodstuffs, the distribution thereof will be stopped."

* * *

The city council of Warsaw at a meeting on October 3, 1945, was informed by the government that the cities of Olsztyn (Allenstein), Elblag (Elbing) and Szczecin (Stettin) were designated for the settlement of Warsaw's excess population living amid the capital's devastation. It was reported that 25,000 Warsaw residents had registered for resettlement in the newly-acquired Oder area, although many already had left on their own, regretting it later.

* * *

The Russians lost no time in reconstructing a war-damaged apartment into what is probably the most beautifully furnished embassy in all Europe. The Soviet embassy in Warsaw is a grayish, cement-blocked five-story structure containing from 30 to 40 rooms. Among the furnishings are deep red rugs and carpets, expensive crystal chandeliers, valuable paintings, handsome desks, comfortable chairs and beds. I observed that the Russian embassy is closely guarded by heavily armed Russian troops. While the Russian ambassador, Wiktor Z. Lebiediev, lived in such great splendor, the American ambassador, Arthur Bliss Lane, had very inadequate accommodations in the already overcrowded Polonia Hotel, where most of the embassy staff and foreign correspondents also lived in rooms without bathing or toilet facilities.

KRAKOW

It was a chilly night when a small boy about 8 years old stopped me and an American soldier chauffeur on a busy Krakow street. "Prosze o pare groszy," ("I beg you for a few pennies, please") pleaded the boy, whose bare feet were muddy and his face streaked with dirt. We reached into our pockets and handed him 20 zlotys (20c) each. "Bog zaplac" ("May God repay you"), said the boy as he dashed with joy for home.

* * *

Gasoline—called benzine in Poland—is purchasable only in the black market in Krakow. Sellers demand and get 60 zlotys (60c) per liter (quart) or 240 zlotys ($2.40) per gallon. This writer saw a crowd of 200 Poles watch a black-market operator pour 10 gallons of gasoline into an automobile from two "Jerry" cans. The motorist paid 2,400 zlotys ($24.00 at the official money exchange rate) for the gasoline. Every purchaser of benzine whiffs the contents of the "Jerry" can before he allows the black-market operator to pour it into the tank, lest the stuff be water rather than gasoline.

* * *

Polish hospitals are in extremely poor condition and in dire need of equipment, medicines and doctors. I observed the condition of Bonifratres Hospital in Krakow, when I visited Wincenty Witos, 72, "grand old man" of the Peasant party, shortly before he died. Witos was in a coma at the time and unable to talk with me. A nephew who slept in a cot in the same room served as nurse to Witos. He explained that "Uncle Witos' condition turned for the worse in the morning." Six days later, on October 31, 1945, Witos died. His death was attributed to pneumonia. Impressive funeral rites were held for Witos at Krakow and Wieszchoslawice, where he had lived on a farm before going to the hospital.

* * *

Krakow remains as enchanting as it has in the past, except for nominal destruction on the outskirts, its blown bridges and demolition of its modern airport and railroad station by the Germans. While Warsaw is depressing and in almost total ruins, I found Krakow gay and refreshing, with its century-old buildings majestically rising in the sky. With the departure of the Germans, the Poles in Krakow quickly changed their street names into Polish "ulicas" and "alejas" from the German names imposed on the streets by the invaders. The Poles boasted proudly to me that their city was the "little Rome" because of the 49 Catholic churches in Krakow.

* * *

Although there was an 11 p.m. daily curfew in the fall of 1945, night clubs, dances, theaters, opera houses and cafes were operating in typical Polish fashion in Krakow. As in Warsaw, gunfire frequently awakened the people of Krakow from their sound sleep at night. A gun duel was staged one night right in front of the Francuski Hotel. Exchanging shots were Polish men and Russian soldiers.

* * *

The unfortunate people of Krakow take off their hats whenever they spot an American. They also congregate around an American automobile and gape with wonderment, for some of them have never before seen an American-made automobile.

* * *

Numerous stores are operating in Krakow, selling almost every conceivable item, including items that were difficult to purchase during the war in America. The latest type of Leica cameras, brand new, were being sold in Krakow at $85, whereas in America, if you could find one, they sold at $285 each. Films and electrical appliances, such as flat irons and heaters, could be purchased in abundance. One British correspondent, Charles Lambert, bought a dozen zippers in Krakow because he told me, "You cannot buy zippers in London."

* * *

On the whole, the Poles in Krakow appear to be better dressed than those in Warsaw, although some appeared to be ragged because the Germans plundered Krakow as they did every Polish city, town and village they invaded, even when they did not destroy it.

* * *

The "hejnal," sound of the Polish trumpeter forbidden by the Germans during the occupation, is again heard every hour from the tower of Mariacki (St. Mary's Church) in the heart of Krakow. The "hejnal" ends abruptly on the quavering note that marked the death so many, many centuries ago of a youthful Polish trumpeter while watching for approaching enemies. According to the story, a Tartar shot an arrow into the trumpeter's throat.

* * *

Postwar Krakow remains the "cultural and newspaper center" of Poland. The Polish Army in August, 1945, completed in that city the first film production in postwar Poland under the strange and mysterious title of "2 x 2 equals 4." The film, shown in movie houses in the fall of 1945, is an animated cartoon illustrating the daily, varied hardships of Polish life. It is a sound movie with dialog, music, voices and noises. The producers admit that it was a crude piece of work, as compared to productions of Fox, Metro-Goldwyn-Mayer or Warner Brothers, but one must not forget that it came into existence out of nothing, for the "shots" were made from animated cartoon sketches drawn with white chalk on a blackboard.   *   *   *

While a guest at a dinner given by the American ambassador, Arthur Bliss Lane, to some of his embassy staff at the Hotel Francuski in Krakow, I heard the ambassador relate how German women and men pleaded with him to spare them from being ousted from their homes in Zabrze, former German city of Hindenburg. Zabrze was annexed to Poland at the end of the war and Ambassador Lane visited it early in October, 1945, as part of his tour of southern Poland.

The Germans in the city of Zabrze wept as they spotted Lane and rushed to him. They protested vigorously that an injustice was being done to them by the Poles, since they were not told where they are going. One woman claimed that she had lived in the United States for 20 years and cried out, "This is Germany from which I'm being driven out."

As the woman was stretching out her hand toward Lane, the ambassador cried out, "Don't put your hands on me. This is Poland. I have been at the embassy in Warsaw for two months. What I saw there where you Germans went from house to house dynamiting, burning and destroying an entire city, is a crime against civilization. I am amazed that any of you Germans can ask for compassion."   *   *   *

POZNAN

A Polish official in Poznan told me that when he protested to a Russian Army officer about acts of vandalism committed by Russian soldiers, the Russian officer countered:

"The trouble with you Poles is that you have too much culture, while we Russians have technique."

* * *

While driving on a Polish highway from Poznan to Warsaw, an American Army officer attached to the American embassy in the Polish capital was suddenly stopped by a Russian Army colonel.

"Give me your tire jack and pump!" demanded the Russian colonel.

"I cannot do that!" countered the American Army officer. "What will I do if I get a flat tire?"

"Do you want to lose your automobile?" cried out the Russian colonel.

Preferring not to be stranded without a car in the uncertain Polish hinterland, the American Army officer surrendered the tire jack and pump to the Russian officer.

This incident, which occurred in the fall of 1945, was reported to the Polish foreign office, which subsequently expressed its "regrets," but did not return the tire jack and pump. The American Army officer was accompanied on the Poznan to Warsaw trip by an American correspondent.

* * *

Fifty men ceased working and rushed around our truck when we stopped in a large Poznan garage to fill our tires with air. Irked by the suspension of work, the boss of the garage crew rushed out of his office and yelled at his men:

"What's the matter with you fellows? Go back to work. Haven't you ever seen people before?"

"Sure we have seen people before," countered one of the gaping workers, a youth, who appeared to be 16. "But these are not just people. These are Americans. I have never seen an American in my life."

The workers continued gaping at us and examining the construction of the truck until we departed. Not until then was any work done on the cars and trucks laid up in the garage lot for repairs.

* * *

Due to the widespread operations of the Russian soldiers and the dreaded NKVD secret police in Poznan in the fall of 1945, the people in that city adhered strictly to the curfew hours. The Poles reported frequent shootings and arrests in this political stronghold of Stanislaw Mikolajczyk, leader of the Polish Peasant party, opponent of the Communist political bloc.

* * *

KOSTRZYN

While riding in a British Army truck through the terribly war-scarred city of Kostrzyn, which the Germans called Kuestrin, two young women stopped us and asked us to take them along anywhere. We told them we could not do that. They told us they wanted to get out of this city. As we drove off, leaving the women behind, I saw four Russian soldiers walking out from the hideous ruins of a building and run after the women. Our truck turned at an intersection and we saw no more of the women and the Russian soldiers.

* * *

SZCZECIN

An observer cannot help noticing the conspicuous absence of dogs in Poland. A young Polish woman who had settled in the newly-acquired Polish port of Szczecin, called Stettin by the Germans, explained that the Germans during the occupation had stolen most of the dogs in Poland and sent them to Germany. She said that the Germans had taken two dogs from her while she lived in Lodz. "Anyone who failed to turn in his dogs to the Germans would be shot," she said.

* * *

Throughout my journey from Warsaw to Szczecin I saw Russian soldiers leading vast herds of cattle and horses eastward toward Russia. There likewise were seemingly endless caravans of horse-drawn wagons loaded with miscellaneous materials traveling in an eastern direction. Aboard these wagons were Russian soldiers armed in many instances with "tommy guns" and "sub-machine guns."

* * *

OKOCIM

Late in October a celebration was held on the occasion of opening the railway line to the Okocim brewery, which the Germans destroyed for a distance of more than five kilometers. Besides the brewery, Okocim has a brickkiln, a marmalade factory, a sawmill and a yeast factory. I drank Okocim beer at the Polonia Hotel in Warsaw. Instead of metal caps, the brewery uses corks in sealing bottle beer. Waiters pull out the corks when the beer is served and put them back into the bottles after they are emptied for re-use by the breweries. There is an acute shortage of facilities to make metal caps in Poland.

* * *

GDYNIA

While in Gdynia on October 28, 1945, I observed happy Poles marching, singing and listening to speeches in celebration of the "Polish Sea Holiday," marking the return to the Polish Navy of the submarines, *Sep*, *Rys*, and *Zbik*, the vessel *Batory*, and the navy's training schooner, *Dar Pomorze*. These submarines, the vessel and the schooner were all returned from Sweden, where they had been interned since the first days of the war in 1939. The *Dar Pomorze* was gaily decorated with colorful pennants and flags.

* * *

SOPOT

The main attraction in this famous resort town, which under German rule was called Zoppot, is the devastated gambling joint called Casino. A Polish woman who had lived there through the German occupation stated that the tall, white Casino had attracted many of the "big-shot" Nazis who "relaxed from their job of killing Poles by gambling for high stakes." A narrow-gauge railroad track has been constructed to the entrance of the Casino to haul away the rubble from the former "palace of gamblers."

* * *

GDANSK

Streetcars are operating in all important Polish cities, but none of the streetcars are as decorative as those in

Gdansk, the former "Free City of Danzig." The streetcars in this town are in excellent shape and painted a
rich white, with gold lettering. Gdansk for the most part
has hideous ruins, but the streetcars are really something
to ride. The contrast is refreshing.

* * *

LODZ

Automobiles operated by the Poles are chiefly German-
produced and in extremely poor condition. They are
considerably smaller than American-made cars. It is
amazing the high speeds they are being driven around the
battle-scarred countryside. That explains why there are
so many accidents and breakdowns of these cars. Not
having driven automobiles for a number of years, the
Poles fail to appreciate the danger in driving these cars
in such reckless manner. I saw many accidents involving
these cars while touring Poland. One Polish motorist
drove at such a high rate of speed over a long, winding
bridge near Lodz that his little car went right through
the wooden railing and dropped some 40 feet into a deep
river. Special courses in driving were being advertised
in Lodz.

* * *

CZESTOCHOWA

Contrary to popular belief in America, the miraculous
picture, which depicts the Blessed Virgin and Infant
Jesus with dark complexions, was not seized by the
Germans from Jasna Gora at Czestochowa—Poland's
greatest place of pilgrimage known as the "Mecca of
Poland." Several Pauline Fathers took me on a tour

of this famed shrine and monastery, explaining in detail the history of the institution that has all the earmarks of the Middle Ages.

* * *

The Pauline monastery still possesses a large library, although many of its precious books were carted away by the Germans. A large visitors' book contains the signature of Gestapo Chief Heinrich Himmler, who visited the monastery with a group of his henchmen during the occupation.

* * *

Crippled and infirm Poles flock daily to Jasna Gora to pray before the miraculous picture in the church, which has a tower rising nearly 300 feet, the highest tower in Poland. Scores of crutches and trusses hang in the chapel of the Blessed Virgin in mute evidence of the cures reported to have taken place there. The miraculous picture is studded with precious stones, none of which were removed by the Germans.

* * *

KATOWICE

The people come to Katowice from miles around to obtain coal for the approaching winter. Most of them come with horses and old wagons, which are too heavily loaded and occasionally tip as the driver goes up a steep hill on the highway back to his village or farm. I saw men and women carry on their backs for some miles long wicker baskets or burlap bags loaded with 100 or 200 pounds of coal. Many Polish women dig for coal alongside railroad tracks.

XIII

UNRRA GOODS ON THE BLACK MARKET

Many UNRRA articles, intended for distribution among undernourished Poles, found their way into the Polish black markets. Repeated charges were also made by Poles in the hinterland that the UNRRA goods were used for political purposes in an effort to persuade the Poles to join the Communist Polish Workers' party or the newly-communized Polish Socialist party, which follows the Red party line.

UNRRA relief goods arriving in Poland in the summer and fall of 1945 were all turned over to the respective Polish ministries for distribution among the Poles, according to C. S. Anderson, Professor of Education at Pennsylvania State College, on leave, who was the requirements-and-supply specialist of the UNRRA Polish mission stationed in the Polonia Hotel in Warsaw. For example, he said the Ministry of Health received the shipments of medicines, hospital equipment, etc., and the Ministry of Agriculture received the shipments of farm implements, seeds, etc.

Just where and how the Polish ministries distributed the UNRRA relief goods in the fall of 1945 was not determined.

"UNRRA receives no records from these various Polish ministries to show where or how the UNRRA

relief commodities have been distributed in Poland,"
Anderson said in October, 1945, in Warsaw. "Consequently, we have no knowledge of the final disposition of
the UNRRA goods once they are turned over to the ministries."

The fact that politics entered into the distribution of
UNRRA goods cannot be denied. The government newspaper, *Zycie Warszawy*, in its October 28, 1945, issue
announced the "control over distribution of UNRRA
goods" as follows: "On the 26th a commission for the
control over the distribution of UNRRA goods met. It
is composed of representatives of the political parties,
trade unions, Spolem (a co-operative), the municipal
provisioning department and the UNRRA. The 'Spolem'
storehouses were inspected."

Many Poles, including a Polish newspaper reporter
who cannot work on a newspaper because he does not
belong to the "Red Party," stated that persons belonging
to the Polish Workers party or the Polish Socialist party
received preferential ration cards entitling them to
UNRRA relief goods. They explained that ration cards
in Poland were divided into some five categories, and that
those who refused to align themselves with the Polish
Workers' party or the Polish Socialist party received the
"lowest type of ration cards" which entitled them to
"practically nothing."

Sales of UNRRA goods in the black market, where
they were sold at exorbitant prices were common. I have
seen these goods sold all over Poland, including the
Warsaw black market. Lux soap was sold right in front
of the Polonia Hotel in Warsaw at 90 zlotys (90c) a bar
and American canned salmon at from 150 to 300 zlotys
($1.50 to $3.00 a can).

Vigorous objections to abuses of UNRRA gifts shipped to Poland were expressed by the editors of even the *Dziennik Ludowy* (The People's Daily), which is the voice of the leftist faction of the Peasants' party. In its October 3, 1945, edition, it said editorially:

"Every now and then we read in the press: 'An UNRRA ship has arrived in Gdynia' and further that it brought so and so much food as cocoa, coffee, cheeses, sardines, condensed milk, chocolate, canned fruit.

"When a person reads this his heart beats with joy; he imagines how he will eat these excellent things. Meanwhile one convoy after another arrives; first they came from far away Constanza through Rumania and we were vaguely informed that the distance was great (because it was Rumania), and the food spoiled. At last cynically we were told that they were sold in order to buy something nourishing, because, it is known that the peasant, worker and office worker will not know how to judge such good things. Instead, he will receive one more 'card'—bread.

"Now the ships arrive in Gdynia. The Ministry of Food and Commerce has published that nothing is sold out of UNRRA goods on the free market, that there are more and more so-called 'luxury' goods and our mouths continue to water as they did, and nothing promises to bring a change.

"And here there can be no explanation or avoiding the point. We read the official news that UNRRA is sending us those goods; we see them in shops in Gdynia, in Warsaw and in all large Polish cities. They just lie in the shop windows and a person takes a look at them. If he is calm he sighs, if he is more excitable he frowns and goes on.

"The prices are sky-high so only the 'speculators' can

permit themselves those 'luxuries' and they are the only ones who are full of praise for UNRRA.

"Is the purpose of those gifts really only to satisfy the whims of profiteers, speculators, pilferers or ordinary thieves of the public funds?

"How does it happen—the worker asks—that so-called luxury goods are not distributed, nor sold and yet every shop has them?

"The answer presents itself: Only through theft. We want the Ministry of Food and Commerce to answer all those doubts of the working man, that it should at last be explained whether they are sold on the free market, which we consider inadmissible as favoring the speculator at the expense of the working man.

"It seems to us that somebody should be locked up, and for a long time. And if there are thefts, let the goods coming from theft be confiscated and the culprits be punished!"

On October 11, 1945, the same Leftist newspaper stated in a story headlined "THIEVES ARE STEALING UNRRA GOODS":

"A number of persons plundered the *SS. Oremar* on September 27. Many goods were taken out of cartons and off the ship without anybody restraining the robbers. The same is happening during the daytime, and the crews take documentary pictures of this procedure. This was established by the chief of the Propaganda Section in Gdynia."

Following the publication of such editorials and news items, the editors of *Dziennik Ludowy* in their October 22, 1945, issue, printed the following "publishers' declaration":

"This paper wrote often about abuses in the distribution of foodstuffs from storehouses. As none of the public offices have answered these accusations, this paper will in the future notify the Supreme Chamber of National Control of all abuses."

Dr. Jerzy Sztachelski, Minister of Food and Trade, declared early in October, 1945:

"Our food situation is bad, and winter may prove difficult. UNRRA supplies of food are small. Russia is helping us somewhat. In September, 1945, we obtained 30,000 tons of flour from Russia."

Dr. Sztachelski, who has control over the distribution of food in Poland, is a member of the Communist Polish Workers' party. He showered no praise on the United States for the millions of dollars worth of UNRRA relief sent to poverty-stricken Poland. His praise was limited to Russia.

There was no telephone communication between Warsaw and Gdynia in the fall of 1945. Consequently, UNRRA officials were compelled to make frequent trips over poor roads to Gdynia to keep in touch and check up on UNRRA relief ships arriving there from the United States before the goods were transferred to the Polish ministries for distribution.

The Poles crowded around every UNRRA automobile in sight while en route to or from Gdynia in the hope of getting fats and bacon. They were extremely disappointed to learn that the automobiles, bearing UNRRA lettering, had nothing to distribute to them, for the relief goods were all turned over to the Polish ministries.

A number of foreign UNRRA officials in Warsaw expressed disgust at the distribution setup. Polish government officials had complained about the lack of trucks needed to distribute UNRRA goods to needy Poles, but there were hundreds of idle trucks parked in vast areas fenced off by the Russian Army.

Poland is truly poor and in dire need of UNRRA assistance.

"Americans must not overlook the fact that Poland actually went through three wars rather than just one since 1939," Anderson said. "The first war was when Germany and Russia invaded Poland. The second, when the Poles conducted their unsuccessful insurrection against the Germans in 1944, and the third when the Russians swept through Poland to drive out the Germans. These three wars ground Poland to the earth, stripping it of its homes, personal possessions, barns, livestock, farm implements, cattle, horses and industrial machinery."

What does the average Pole need most in these critical postwar days?

Anderson replied:

"First, the average Pole needs a pair of shoes. It is startling, but the fact remains that only 20% of the Poles have adequate shoes, according to our UNRRA survey. The Germans, according to the survey, stripped the Poles of their footwear in 1939, and would not allow any leather to be imported in Poland for the production of new shoes. Poland is not a leather producer. Consequently, the Poles were unable to replace their worn-out shoes. The few remaining Poles who have shoes do not wear them while walking out in the country. Instead, they walk barefooted until they come to the city. Then they put on their shoes. Every Pole who has shoes uses them sparingly.

"Other items urgently needed by the Poles are ready-to-wear garments, raw cotton and wools for the existing textile mills in Poland, semifabricated materials, yarns, yard goods, fats—lard, backfat, cod liver oil, margarine, cotton seed oil—soap, bulk condensed whole milk and dry skimmed milk and medical supplies, such as hospital equipment, beds, furnishings, instruments, penicillin and sulfa drugs."

The UNRRA was continuing to bring in all these items into Poland from the United States in the fall of 1945, but no one saw the distribution of these articles on any large scale. The future of Poland depended on the distribution of those articles. The Poles cannot keep on going as they have been unless those relief goods are distributed to them fairly and honestly regardless of their political party affiliations or political beliefs.

A reliable source in Warsaw informed correspondents, after complaints were made about the sale of UNRRA goods on the free market, that the Ministry of Food and Trade figured the Poles were "unaccustomed to such luxury foods" as prunes, canned meats and fruits and therefore placed 50 tons of UNRRA goods on the open market. This source explained that the ministry intended to use the funds derived from the sale to purchase beans, peas and other staple foods and then deliver these goods to the Polish workers.

UNRRA officials in Warsaw told the ministry that they looked with keen disfavor upon any such scheme and the ministry had promised to discontinue selling such goods on the open market. This practice continued, however.

XIV

NO FREEDOM OF THE PRESS

I found no freedom of the press in Poland. Newspapers, as well as all mail sent through the Polish post office, were strictly censored.

News cabled direct from Warsaw in the fall of 1945 was also subject to strict censorship regulations of the Polish provisional government. Foreign correspondents "smuggled" their dispatches out of Poland or wrote them after leaving Poland to avoid censorship of their copy.

The official Polish news-gathering agency is known as PAP (Polska Agencja Prasowa), formerly Polpress. PAP articles are as common in Polish newspapers as the AP (Associated Press) articles in American newspapers. The big difference, however, is that PAP articles contain only information favorable to or bearing the approval of the Polish puppet government.

Although some 300 newspapers and scores of other periodicals were being published in postwar Poland in the fall of 1945, the editors of these publications could not run articles and editorials as freely as the editors of newspapers do in America.

Roman Szydlowski, Jewish editor of the *Polish Monthly Review* and chief censor of Krakow, which is the publishing center of Poland, told me that press censorship was the result of the "current unstable conditions and exists for the welfare of the new Polish nation."

"Not all items can be published because some of them might be detrimental to internal security," said Szydlowski, who made no bones about his Communist party affiiliations. "It is for that reason that censorship must prevail."

Poland's No. 1 newspaperman and publisher is Jerzy Borejsza, director of Czytelnik, a powerful Leftist publishing co-operative organized with the establishment of the Polish provisional government.

Boresjsza was a left wing journalist and writer long before the war. When the war broke out in 1939, he was in Lwow. He later went to Moscow, entered the Polish Army there and fought as a major on the battle fronts. Following the liberation of Poland, he became director of Czytelnik.

About 20% to 25% of the publications in Poland are put out by Czytelnik. This co-operative publishes 18 dailies, at least one in each large Polish community.

The leading newspapers published in Warsaw are:

Rzeczpospolita (Republic), government daily designated also for Lodz, Krakow and Lublin; *Kuryier Codzienny* (Daily Courier), which serves as the voice of the Polish Democratic party; *Glos Ludu* (Voice of the People), daily of the Polska Partia Robotnicza (Polish Workers' party); *Zycie Warszawy* (Life of Warsaw), which is published by Czytelnik; and *Dziennik Ludowy* (People's Daily), which is the voice of the Peasant party.

Since the arrival of foreign correspondents in Poland, the government press has repeatedly published editorials sharply criticizing their dispatches in an effort to intimidate the correspondents.

The editorials, written in the style of Russia's communistic "*Pravda*" newspaper, accused the correspondents of "grossly misrepresenting" conditions and thereby "harming the relations" between nations. One of the most sharply-worded editorials appeared October 16, 1945, in the *Dziennik Polski*. Entitled "Straight in the Eyes: To the Foreign Correspondents in Poland," the editorial read in part:

"The foreign press, especially that from the distant west, makes horrible reports on eastern Europe, where polar bears walk on the streets and where men in sable coats drive, in the company of seductive women in carriages drawn by three horses. It would seem that the world cataclysm had finished once and for all with that kind of stories, but it seems that they are immortal. For what else, but a kind of bear and troika story are the various new, amazing revelations of foreign correspondents staying in Warsaw, that are published in English, American and French press.

"What do we learn from them? In the streets of Warsaw there is shooting and dancing; at night regular battles take place; thousands of soldiers and thousands of blonde girls take part in these battles, and when the salvos cease there is the roar of an exploding German mine. And at the same time one sees everywhere queues of paupers, waiting to obtain a bowl of evil-smelling soup, etc., etc. And the *New York Times* tells how 'the Polish secret police, the so-called SPB, organizes man hunts in order to catch anti-communistic elements.'"

While tons of UNRRA goods from the United States were turned over to the various Polish ministries for free distribution among the Poles, the government-controlled press seldom wrote about this assistance. Instead, the press constantly editorialized on "great shipments of food and wearing apparel arriving in Poland from Russia."

The government-controlled press likewise editorialized on the "freedom of workers in Russia" as compared to the "enslavement of workers in America." Samples of such editorializing from the October 3, 1945, issue of *Glos Ludu* follows:

"After the feast of victory over Japan, hundreds of thousands of workers in America returned to the closed gates of their factories. In one day in New York more than 200,000 workers lost their jobs. In the automobile and airplane industries, the number of employed workers fell from 2,500,000 to 700,000. The epidemic of unemployment is spreading in the United States in a terrifying manner.

"Millions of workers in the United States are facing destitution. Those who are still working are gripped by fear and insecurity.

"The press, which is under the control of the industrial concerns, advises the unemployed not to remain in large industrial centers, where there will not be any work for some time to come."

The editorial, entitled "The Normal Condition of Capitalistic Economy," quoted *The Daily Worker* (New York organ of the American Communist party) as saying:

"The reaction aims to disperse the workers in all of the country. It wants the workers to starve at home in silence."

Thus, in typical *Pravda* (Moscow newspaper) manner, the Russian puppet government in Poland is using its newspapers to spread Soviet falsehoods about Americans and the American way of life.

A Polish journalist, who cannot work now on a newspaper because he is not a member of the Communist party, stated:

"While you see many newspapers in Poland, not one of them is free. The editors can only publish what the government tells them. The present government leaders are not representatives of the people. They are hand picked by Moscow. The government ridicules foreign correspondents because it does not believe in a free press.

"Nobody in Poland had ever heard of President Boleslaw Bierut and Prime Minister Edward Osobka Morawski until Moscow announced them as leaders of the new provisional government of Poland.

"Secret police are operating everywhere in Poland today. Poles who are overheard criticizing the government are arrested and sent away. Nobody hears of them again.

"Poland today is controlled by Russia. America should know that fact."

This journalist said that 90% of the Poles are opposed to the present regime in Poland.

While in Warsaw, I roomed with four other correspondents in the Polonia Hotel, which was jammed with diplomats, naval and military personnel, UNRRA officials, journalists from various countries and foreigners with miscellaneous missions.

One day—about the middle of October—a porter brought a note to my room. The note, addressed to one of the correspondents, Gladwin Hill of *The New York Times*, read:

"Dear Glad: Must see you immediately. Meet me in lobby. I fear for your life."

Hill, who had occupied a bed in my room, had boarded an American embassy supply plane for Berlin shortly before the note was brought to my room. The unsealed note appeared to be scribbled rapidly in pencil and signed by an undecipherable name. Oddly enough, Hill was the target of bitter criticism in the Polish press the following few days—after the delivery of the note—as his Berlin-written dispatches about Poland appeared in *The New York Times*.

Hill had traveled extensively in Poland in a Polish government automobile with Oscar Lange, Polish ambassador to the United States, and had noted the same terror, Russian thievery and lack of freedom that I had noted throughout my tour into the war-scarred Polish hinterland.

When I left Poland at the expiration of my Polish visa, a press service correspondent bid me farewell and commented: "You can tell the whole story once you get out of Poland. I've got to stay here."

Due to the strict censorship, most foreign correspondents in the fall of 1945 waited until they were safely away from Poland before writing the results of their investigation and sending their copy to their respective newspapers. The strict censorship in Poland prevailed despite the repeated objections voiced by the American and British embassies that freedom of press was a condition of the Potsdam agreement.

The Potsdam agreement, announced August 2, 1945, stated in part:

". . . and that representatives of the Allied press shall enjoy full freedom to report to the world upon developments in Poland before and during the elections."

* * *

The Soviet-sponsored Polish provisional government in December, 1946, clamped down an additional press restriction by barring from Poland 17 American Polish language newspapers on the grounds that they were "too vehement" in their criticism of the provisional government. These 17 publications included most of the important Polish papers published in America.

Long before the restrictions on the American Polish language newspapers was announced, the Polish provisional government refused to grant clearance into Poland to an American assigned by UNRRA to a public relations position. After waiting months for his Polish visa, the American was informed that no visa would be granted him because his deceased father as editor of an American Polish language newspaper had been unfriendly to Russia.

XV

INTIMIDATING UNITED STATES CITIZENS

Intimidation of United States citizens in Poland by the NKVD, the Polish Militia or Russian soldiers was not an uncommon occurrence.

A number of United States citizens who had appeared at the consulate for repatriation had not only been intimidated, but also beaten by security police and warned not to return in the future to the consulate. One day as I watched a man file his repatriation application, he asked a consulate aide in a trembling voice: "Won't anything happen to me for coming here?" The consulate aide expressed regret that he could not assure him security.

The Warsaw consulate, a former private residence, was busy as a beehive from morning to night in the fall of 1945. Set about 25 feet behind a closely guarded gate with a "peephole," the consulate building—painted a creamy color—is overgrown partly by thick ivy reaching from ground to roof. A large flock of tiny birds flutter in and out of the ivy, chirping a "song of hope" for the war sufferers claiming to be citizens of the United States and pleading to be returned to it as soon as possible.

The atmosphere around the consulate was in sharp contrast to the nearby debris and demolished buildings, where there were neither leaves nor birds. The consulate was renovated at considerable expense to the United States government.

Several thousand American citizens, who lived through the harrowing German occupation, had filed applications for repatriation to America within a few weeks after the re-establishment of the United States embassy in Warsaw in the summer of 1945.

Every applicant had to await investigation by the United States immigration authorities to determine citizenship validity. Many of the applicants were men who had fought with the American Army in the first World War and had settled in Poland, receiving an American pension on which, though it was modest according to United States standards, they lived comfortably in Poland. They never became naturalized Poles.

Americans wishing to return to the United States and in need of aid, were given immediate financial assistance at the consulate, provided they brought with them documents sufficient for the issuance of a passport. A complete investigation of their citizenship claims and right to repatriation followed. A check of the American citizens filing repatriation applications disclosed that most of them have been born in or have relatives in Chicago, Milwaukee, Buffalo, Detroit, Jersey City, St. Louis, Scranton, or New York.

Many sad cases involving American citizens may be found in the files of the Warsaw consulate.

For example, one middle-aged woman had walked a long distance to the Warsaw consulate to present her claim as a United States citizen.

She stated that her husband was killed by the Germans in their home when he produced his United States passport to the invaders. The shooting took place, she said, in the presence of their small boy, now 8 years old. She added that her boy developed a foot infection some months ago for lack of shoes. Consequently, she sadly explained, she had to carry him around on her back.

Consulate employees said that this woman had a valid claim to United States citizenship and financial assistance was given her pending repatriation.

Another woman, claiming to have been born in Chicago, came to the consulate from a small village near the Czecho-Slovakian border. She wore a floral scarf around her head. Her black coat was threadbare and covered with dust. She wore military shoes, men's heavy gray woolen socks and a dress of thin material. She stated that the slow train ride took her 20 hours to come to Warsaw. Although she had numerous papers with her in a yellowed envelope, she did not have the required documents attesting to her citizenship. She was advised to return to her home and write to Chicago for her birth certificate. She broke into tears.

One man who confided he was yearning to go to the United States stated: "Poland has been the unhappiest place in the world throughout my life. When I was 12, there was a bloody outbreak here. When I was 20, I went into the army for eight years. When I was 45, the second World War broke out and cleaned me out completely, except for the clothes I'm wearing. If I am ever able to get back on my feet, I'll try to go to America. If I cannot get to America, I'll try to go to Australia."

Ambassador Lane stated that the arrival of American correspondents in Poland was the most important factor in clearing the atmosphere, as between the United States and the new Polish nation.

"Some of the information which the correspondents sent to their newspapers may not have been favorable to the Polish provisional government," said Lane, "but at least the American people are in a position now to know the truth whether it is good or bad, just as the rest of the world is entitled to know what is good or bad in the United States."

In his extensive travels Lane has especially concentrated on a study of conditions in Gdynia, Gdansk, Lublin, Krakow, Czestochowa, Katowice, Oswiecim, Wroclaw and Lodz.

Other embassy officials have also traveled through Poland to note postwar conditions. While in Krakow, an embassy official was approached by a boy, about 12, who inquired whether he was Col. York (Lt. Col. Edward J. York, attached to the United States embassy in Warsaw as Ambassador Lane's pilot).

"No, I'm not Col. York," replied the official, "but maybe I can help you."

"Well, I don't know if you can," said the boy. "My parents wanted to talk about their American citizenship to Col. York and the chance they have of returning to America."

"Getting back United States citizens to America is part of my job," replied the embassy official. "Why don't you have them come here to see me? I'll be in this city for a few days."

"Oh, no, they can't come to see you," said the boy, "because they are afraid they may be arrested for coming here to talk with you."

This incident illustrates the fear under which United States citizens are living in postwar Poland.

Even Americans attached to the United States embassy have been molested by Russian soldiers and the Soviet-commanded Polish militiamen. On a number of occasions Russian soldiers stopped American embassy cars on the highways in Poland and demanded transportation under threat. One embassy clerk said that a Polish militiaman fired several shots at his automobile late at night in Warsaw even though the automobile was distinctly designated as an American vehicle with an American flag. When this embassy clerk stopped his car and requested an explanation of the gunfire, one of the group of Polish militiamen said, "We're sorry!"

Because of such promiscuous shooting on the part of "trigger happy" Polish militiamen, the Americans attached to the United States embassy for the most part confined themselves at night to their rooms in the Polonia Hotel or in the "embassy club room." This "club room," in addition to being used for recreational purposes, served also as quarters for unexpected visitors or supply plane pilots who stayed overnight. One night some 20 Americans congregated in this tiny "club room." Two couples were dancing while a phonograph was playing Harry James's records. An army major was dictating to a sergeant seated at a typewriter. A group of girls were reading magazines and books. Another girl was sewing up a "run" in her stocking. Two men were reading month-old copies of *"The Stars and Stripes."* And two other men were setting up cinema equipment to show movies for a couple of hours, including *Iwo Jima* in reverse because this was viewed so many times by the movie-hungry American embassy employees.

"Grand Central Station" was the name given to the room occupied by Stephen B. Jenkins, 37, a former Milwaukeean, in the embassy quarters in the Polonia Hotel in Warsaw.

A state department employee since November, 1942, Jenkins served in Washington, Buenos Aires, Lima, Santiago and London before coming with Ambassador Lane and a staff of 12 to Warsaw on July 31, 1945. Jenkins knew just what to take along with him to Warsaw. Consequently, all state department employees rushed to his room for such items as screwdrivers, hammers, plates, knives, forks, lighting and cleaning fluids, tomato soup. The comings-and-goings led to the calling of his room "Grand Central Station."

Because of the enormous stock of supplies he carries with him wherever he goes, Jenkins traveled to Poland with several trunks.

"Of all the places in which I served as a state department employee," Jenkins told me, "I found conditions worst in Warsaw. We knew before we came that this would not be a bed of roses. But it's worse than we expected. This is the first time that the state department had to set up headquarters under such adverse conditions. The Poles greeted us Americans with tears in their eyes when we arrived in July."

Secret police agents kept a constant watch on foreigners, particularly Americans and Britons, and on Poles who were seen greeting or talking to any Americans or Englishmen. The Poles took a great risk in talking to Americans and Britishers because in many instances they were arrested and detained in jail for gruelling questioning as to their conversations with foreigners.

Throughout my travels in Poland I had to surrender my passport to the clerks in the hotels, where I was staying. The clerks apologized for the inconvenience by stating that they had to turn over the passports for a day or two to the secret police for a checkup. One hotel clerk whispered to me: "We Poles wish that the Russian soldiers and the NKVD would leave Poland so that we could operate this hotel freely without interference and such regulations as they impose on us."

Americans were not immune from arrest by the secret police. In the fall of 1945 the secret police detained a United States Army sergeant, Louis Nagy of Walton, W. Va. He was freed through the intervention of American military authorities after five months' detention. Nagy said he was half starved by the secret police, whom he accused of beating and questioning him scores of times.

Immediately upon arrival in any Polish city, town or village, the American visitor stopping at a hotel was visited by a "reporter" from a Polish government newspaper and asked: "What is your purpose in visiting Poland? Why did you come to this community? What are you going to do here? What do you think of our new democracy?" The Communist-led Polish government enforced the brutal doctrine that "the end justifies the means" in promoting Communism in Poland and did not want the "means" disclosed to American correspondents by the average Poles, who risked their lives talking to the correspondents.

* * *

On the eve of the fake elections held in Poland January 19, 1947, the American embassy in Warsaw was investigating the sudden arrest by Polish security police of 100 Poles who claimed American citizenship. Charges against the prisoners were not disclosed, and the embassy immediately started to negotiate with the Polish regime for their release.

"Where to?"

XVI

POLAND IS A LESSON FOR AMERICAN DIPLOMACY

American Communists and their "fellow travelers" are loud exponents of the expanding Russian dictatorship, but none of them cares to pack up their belongings and settle behind the iron curtain that has fallen in Central and Eastern Europe. Instead, they remain in the United States to take full advantage of the freedom that is denied millions of people in Soviet-occupied countries, including Poland, and spread lying propaganda.

Freedom, as we know it in America, is priceless. The Polish nation has fought centuries for freedom because of its geographical misfortune in having a vice-like location between Germany and Russia. Hitler started the World War II in Poland. Stalin aided and abetted Hitler in enslaving Poland. These are undeniable historical facts. Because of its suffering, no nation deserves more sympathy and help than Poland. Yet freedom has not returned to Poland, despite the volumes of Moscow propaganda and the propaganda of American Communists and their fellow travelers that "a new democracy has come to Poland."

The insidious, false Communist propaganda about the "new democracy" in Poland has spread in America like a cancerous growth, even affecting some newspapermen who have not been behind the iron curtain to see for themselves the true conditions among peoples enslaved by Soviet Russia. It apparently was far "easier" for these blinded newspapermen to swallow the sugar-coated Communist line than to face the bitter truth about the aftermath of World War II. One newspaperman, upon my return from Poland, commented, "Why don't the Poles get smart and take on Communism. It is the coming thing."

I told the reporter that since he did not live under Russian domination he knew nothing about the Communist way of life as compared to the American way of life and therefore should not wish something unto others that he himself would not like. I pointed out to him how I had to smuggle my news dispatches out of Poland, how the dreaded NKVD secret police break into the homes of Poles at all hours of the day and night, how the people of Poland live in constant fear and terror and how the war-scarred Polish nation is ruled by a puppet government in which they have neither a voice nor representation.

Freedom-loving Americans must and should face the facts in the case of Poland, the gallant little nation that bore the brunt of Hitler's Blitzkrieg in 1939, for Poland remains Europe's worst danger spot despite the defeat of Hitler and Nazism.

Every American should be on guard against the lying propaganda of Communists who camouflage themselves as "defenders of democracy." "Democracy" under Communism means the destruction of the basic freedoms of mankind as guaranteed in the American bill of rights. Communism, like "facism" and "Nazism," breeds hatreds, bigotry and disunity. It despises truthful, objective reporting.

The government-controlled press in Poland constantly rebuked American correspondents for writing their dispatches in the typically American objective manner. That explains why so few correspondents are given permission to enter Poland. The Soviet-sponsored regime in Poland does not want objective reporting to disclose what is going on behind the iron curtain. Communism thrives on sugar-coated propaganda, not on truth.

American diplomacy has been extremely outmaneuvered by Russia in the case of Poland. Though freedom of press in Poland was agreed upon at Potsdam, the Polish provisional government clamped on a rigid censorship.

American diplomacy has likewise been unsuccessful in putting an end to the operations of the dreaded NKVD and the Russian Army garrisons in Poland.

Under the Yalta Conference, "free and unfettered" elections in Poland were promised, but the Polish provisional government began preparations for election day by establishing an armed citizens' voluntary reserve militia under the pretext that this militia will assure "peaceful and orderly balloting." This militia, called "Ormo," has recruited some 100,000 armed men, chiefly members of the Communist Polish Workers' party and its collaborating Polish Socialist party. Hitler had established a similar militia in Germany for "election purposes."

The source of all the trouble in postwar Poland can definitely be traced back to Yalta when Stalin was given a free rein by Great Britain and America to establish his sphere of influence in the Baltic republics, Poland and Rumania.

Poland will continue being Europe's worst danger spot until the Allies undo the great sacrifice made at Yalta, for the Poles will continue their struggle for freedom and independence, despite what may take place in their country and despite the Communist propaganda that "a new democracy has come to Poland," which is nothing more than a plan to sovietize helpless Poland.

The world has shrunk as a result of speedy air travel. Two World Wars have proven how our armed forces became entangled in international conflicts. The shrinkage of the world will involve the United States even more in problems that are international in scope. For that reason the United States must concentrate more than it ever has in the past on its diplomatic policies and in the training of the men and women who comprise its diplomatic corps. The United States must cease its diplomatic policy of "pussyfooting" in the case of Poland. Repeated concessions made to Russia in the case of Poland are responsible to a great extent for the chaos and lack of freedom in that war-scarred little country.

The United States must recognize that it does have international responsibilities as well as national. Our embassies scattered throughout the world are in a sense our first line of defense, for they serve as our contacts between nations. Great duties are assigned to the men and women working in these embassies. That is why the United States must spend more money than it has in the past for the establishment and maintenance of embassies and for the salaries and training of embassy officials.

Whether we wish to face the fact or not, the sacrifice of Poland at Yalta will long remain a blot in our diplomatic history. Americans are conscious of that fact, particularly the men of our armed forces who fought a bitter war in Europe to oust Hitlerism so that the little nations might be free and truly democratic. Unhappy observers of the tragedies occurring daily in Russian dominated

Poland were a small group of American soldiers assigned to driving and repairing embassy automobiles. The sentiment of these soldiers was expressed by the GI while on a tour of Krakow with me.

"To think that I had been fighting to free Poland and other small nations only to see something like this happen," remarked the GI, who had a Purple Heart for wounds suffered in Germany.

Poland will continue to be a sad country until a truly representative government is established under which there will be no further violation of the right "to life, liberty and the pursuit of happiness." Whether such a government will become a reality for some time to come is doubtful, for Russia is obviously not anxious to have a Polish neighbor that is free, strong and independent.

* * *

The Red Star over Poland became more than just a temporary fixture on January 19, 1947—the date of the farcical, rigged Polish elections, held 17 months after the announcement of the Potsdam agreement, under which the three powers, United States, Britain and Russia, reassured the Polish people that in accordance with the Yalta agreement "free and unfettered" elections would be held in Poland "as soon as possible on the basis of universal suffrage and secret ballot."

Bolstered by hundreds of thousands of Russian troops, thousands of Russian MBD (formerly NKVD) secret police and a vast regular and volunteer militia, the Polish puppet government held the long over-due "elections" without permitting the voters to seal their ballots.

Reports emanating from behind the iron curtain disclosed innumerable election discrepancies that prompted

Stanislaw Mikolajczyk, vice-premier and Polish Peasant party leader, to immediately voice strenuous objections.

The Polish puppet government, however, ignored Mikolajczyk's objections as unofficial returns indicated that the Communist-led bloc parties captured or will control nearly 90% of the 444 seats in the new parliament.

The results of the balloting were no surprise, for the puppet government with the aid of Moscow spent 17 months, since the announcement of the Potsdam agreement, in rigging the elections and liquidating thousands of Mikolajczyk's followers. One of the most important roles in manipulating the elections was assumed by Yakub Berman, under-secretary of the Polish council of ministers. It is said that not even Provisional President Bierut could issue an order without the approval of Berman, who has spent the greater part of his adult life in Russia where he was close to the Kremlin inner circle. Berman is reported to be the only man in the Polish puppet government to have direct wire and telephone connection with Moscow.

Mikolajczyk will go down in Polish history as one of the greatest champions in that country's traditional fight for freedom.

Now that the long anticipated fake elections were finally conducted in Poland what does the future hold in store for Mikolajczyk?

Perhaps the future of Mikolajczyk depends on Berman, who is reported to have said that the future for Mikolajczyk would depend on his (Mikolajczyk's) attitude, adding that "for those who persist in contacts with the underground we will be ruthless." Since Berman is a Moscow authority, the future for Mikolajczyk and millions of other Poles may be "ruthless," for the term "underground" includes persons voicing disapproval of the fake elections and disagreeing with the Communist way of life destined for Poland.

The final vestige of protection which the millions of Poles crying for freedom after victory might have had has vanished with the rigged elections on January 19, 1947.

Criticism of the fake elections was voiced by the United States on January 28, 1947, when the state department issued the following statement:

"The United States government considers that the Polish provisional government has failed to carry out its solemn pledges.

"The United States government firmly intends to maintain its interest in the welfare of the Polish people.

"While retaining full liberty of action to determine its future attitude toward the government of Poland, this government will continue to keep itself informed of developments in Poland through its diplomatic mission in Warsaw.

"The reports received from the United States embassy in Poland in the period immediately prior to the elections, as well as its subsequent reports based upon the observations of American officials who visited a number of Polish voting centers, confirmed the fears which this government had expressed that the election would not be free. These reports were corroborated by the general tenor of the dispatches from foreign correspondents in Poland.

"It is clear that the provisional government did not confine itself to the suppression of the so-called 'underground' but employed widespread measures of coercion and intimidation against democratic elements which were loyal to Poland although not partisans of the government 'bloc.' "

Whether the United States and Britain will be successful in preventing a "ruthless" future for millions of Poles comprising the so-called democratic elements headed by Mikolajczyk is uncertain. What is certain is the fact that the repeated protests voiced by the United States and Britain for 17 months against the decrees, mass arrests and the rigged election preparations of the Polish provisional government, which now has been replaced by a permanent Communist-led government, did prove futile.

What is also certain is the fact that freedom, as defined by Western civilization, will not return to Poland until the RED STAR OVER POLAND vanishes. Until that day comes, the Poles will continue "to cry for freedom after victory."